HEATHER GAUT

The Pilgrim's
STONE

One Woman's Unpredictable and Authentic Journey

The Pilgrim's Stone

By Heather Gauthier BScN, RN, MBA

Copyright © 2017 by Heather R. Gauthier.

All rights reserved. No part of this book may be reproduced by any mechanical, photographic, or electronic process, or in the form of a phonographic recording, nor may it be stored in a retrieval system, transmitted, or otherwise be copied for public or private use – other than for "fair use" as brief quotations embodied in articles and reviews without prior written permission of the author.

In the event that you use any of the information in this book for yourself, which is your constitutional right, the author assumes no responsibility for your actions.

ISBN: 1983897655
ISBN 13: 978-1983897658

Printed in Canada

Editor: Stephanie Cervone
Cover design & interior layout: © Studio 6 Sense LLC
Shell art design: Daryl Graham

For Pilgrim's,
Past, present and future.
May you seek and find balance,
within your body, mind and soul.

Contents

Foreword...ix

A Cancer patient gets inspired by a Pilgrim's honesty and authenticity. She vows to get well enough to walk 780 km on the Camino de Santiago in Gratuity to God for letting her live. A review of the past needs reconciling in order for her to move forward with better alignment to body, mind and soul. A deep desire to be a Pilgrim is the life line that pulls her out of darkness.

Body

The Body portion of the Camino speaks to the physical element of the Pilgrimage. They say that the Camino trail is divided into Body, Mind and Soul; a third of the total kilometres for each section. It is said that the Camino with test a Pilgrim on each aspect until lessons are learned.

CHAPTER 1: Geese..3
CHAPTER 2: Travel Prison 7
CHAPTER 3: Buses and Trains 11
CHAPTER 4: I'm Sure It's Fine 15
CHAPTER 5: Crossing the Pyrenees 21
CHAPTER 6: Duct Tape 25
CHAPTER 7: Ghost Towns 29
CHAPTER 8: Grit 35
CHAPTER 9: Boots 39
CHAPTER 10: Angel of Mercy 43
CHAPTER 11: Soul Shake 47
CHAPTER 12: Dream Bigger 53
CHAPTER 13: Tender, Loving, Care...57
CHAPTER 14: The Pilgrim's Stone 61
CHAPTER 15: Dreams 67

CHAPTER 16: Don't Judge a Book by its Cover 71
CHAPTER 17: Let Go Of Thinking 75

Mind

The Body portion of the Camino speaks to the physical element of the Pilgrimage. They say that the Camino trail is divided into Body, Mind and Soul; a third of the total kilometres for each section. It is said that the Camino with test a Pilgrim on each aspect until lessons are learned.

CHAPTER 18: Self-Sacrifice and EGO 81
CHAPTER 19: Boundaries 85
CHAPTER 20: Closure 93
CHAPTER 21: More Dreams 97
CHAPTER 22: Chemotherapy? 101
CHAPTER 23: Whisper of Thanks 105
CHAPTER 24: The Camino Provides 109

Soul

The Soul aspect of the Pilgrimage begins on the last third of the Camino. It is an unburdening of sin through forgiveness by GOD and of our-selves with a spiritual awakening that brings joyful bliss and fulfilment. It is an earned step and the universal acknowledgement is a feeling of lightness and wellbeing.

CHAPTER 25: I Am a Pilgrim, Not a Hiker 133
CHAPTER 26: Orphaned 139
CHAPTER 27: Tranquility 143
CHAPTER 28: Co's Kiss 147
CHAPTER 29: Survivor Guilt 155
CHAPTER 30: Gerhild 161
CHAPTER 31: No Cochina! 165
CHAPTER 32: Grocery Store Perfume 167
CHAPTER 33: Flavio "The Great" 169

CHAPTER 34: Victory Lap	173
CHAPTER 35: Pilgrim Mass	181
CHAPTER 36: End of the World	185
CHAPTER 37: The Pilgrim's Shell	189
Afterword	195
Special Thanks	197
Bibliography	199
Biography	200
CHAPTER 38: The REAL Last Chapter	201

Foreword

How it all started

Transformation is ugly. It is sometimes that very ugliness that transforms our lives in the best possible way. The pilgrimage started long before I hit the trail. Nearly 5 years prior actually, when during chemotherapy, I was given tickets by a friend to see whatever I wanted at Cinefest. I didn't have much going for me at the time, so free tickets were as good an excuse as any to get out from under my wet blanket of personal chaos for some mental freedom. I carefully selected a documentary called *Las Peregrinas: The Women Who Walk* by a woman named Sue Kenney from Toronto, Ontario who had faced her fears head-on by doing the *Compostela de Santiago* following her own life upheaval. If ever I had needed inspiration, it was then.

As an audience, we waited patiently for the film to begin, but we were waiting for the guest of honour to arrive and she was "walking" late all the way from North Bay. That's a solid 1.5 hour drive from Sudbury. Was she out of her mind? Clearly I hadn't met the likes of Sue Kenney who inspired me on a cellular level, because as soon as she walked into the room, I zoomed in on her smile and hiking boots. I started thinking about my own life's challenges. I already knew I was on the sidelines of my life at the moment; I needed to find my authentic self... whoever that might prove to be, but to be honest, I didn't really know how. I had already read every book on "how to live a simple life" at the Public Library; I meditated on occasion and had been writing a daily gratitude log for years, no matter how grim it's content. It seemed as though there was no end to my personal struggle.

I was in the midst of transitioning back to Canada after having spent the last 10 years of my life in New Mexico and Arizona. I had been working as a Nephrology Nurse while completing my Master's in Business Administration, which in turn led me to an administrative job in New Mexico specializing in dialysis for kidney patients requiring renal replacement therapy. It was good experience and I had a hard-working staff, but I wasn't fulfilled internally. I had married a man who I loved but didn't really know, despite having been dating for three years. He had a lot of well-kept secrets which destroyed my trust and caused me to erupt, either in tears or anger, on a daily basis. I felt trapped and betrayed. The big pieces of my life were all wrong, and with my tail between my legs, I came home to Canada to start again. It was that same year I found a lump on my breast.

My day-to-day life then consisted of breast cancer treatment: two surgeries, chemotherapy, radiation, and five years of an oral medication called Tamoxifen. I felt horrific, ugly, and swollen. I had a ghastly pale yellow hue to compliment my bald head, and a quick death seemed the more pleasant option. I felt far older than my biological years, and life just felt really long and fruitless. Even my laughter sounded strained. I needed a life makeover.

Between the medical appointments and trying to freeze my 34 year-old ovarian eggs, I was officially on sick leave, "due to critical illness". I didn't have a castle of my own to live in anymore, and I was going through a divorce while my waist-length blond hair was falling out. I barely had time to contemplate my possible mortality. I was at the end of my rope physically, mentally, and spiritually. Getting well had proven to be a full time job, so creating an "authentic lifestyle" seemed about as far away as the moon itself.

By the end of the documentary, I was emotionally tilted. The film was honest, and I was moved by this woman's courage to share her deeply personal struggle with the world. I felt like a privileged voyeur. As I left the movie theatre, our eyes met, and she handed me a stone wishing me a "buen Camino". I ran out of the building crying like a child from this simple loving gesture. I was that broken.

I ended up moving like a drifter four times following my return to Canada, until I'd saved enough money for a little cabin on a lake outside of town. Interestingly, every time I moved, I would find that damn stone the pilgrim had given me in one box or another. Stranger still, I borrowed a car from a friend when my jeep was in for repairs and there was a book left on the seat called *My Camino* by Sue Kenney. Well, even the daft couldn't have denied I was being called to walk my own Camino.

I saved my pennies one by one after that day and planned to walk the St. James Way come hell or high water. All I had to do was stay healthy- and things were looking good in that regard. To be perfectly honest, I was hopeless at navigating this pilgrimage with any notable savvy. The journey was the most difficult yet loving thing I had ever done for myself. So, I took a leave of absence from work and planned to walk 800 km as a way to say thank you to the universe for letting me live.

I am not a writer by trade; I'm a nurse, and I had never written anything prior to this that wasn't required by a teacher. Initially, I wrote the strange and beautiful events down in my journal so that I would remember what happened. Now I have to consider that I may be passing the pilgrim's stone on to you. All I can say is I am alive, and I am a pilgrim. We all are.

P.S. "The Journey" by Mary Oliver is my favourite poem. I believe it fits nicely here. Buen Camino!

"The Journey"
By Mary Oliver

One day you finally knew
what you had to do, and began
though the voices around you
kept shouting
their bad advice –
though the whole house
began to tremble
and you felt the old tug
at your ankles
"Mend my life"
each voice cried
But you didn't stop
You knew what you had to do,
Though the wind pried
with its stiff fingers
at the very foundations –
though their melancholy
was terrible.
It was already late
enough, and a wild night,
and the road full of fallen
branches and stones.
But little by little,
as you left their voices behind,
the stars began to burn
through the sheets of clouds,
and there was a new voice,
which you slowly
recognized as your own,
that kept you company
as you strode deeper and deeper
into the world,
determined to do
determined to save
the only life that you could save.

Body

(St. Jean Pied de Port to Burgos)

Section 1 -

BODY: The BODY portion of the Camino speaks to the physical element of the pilgrimage. They say that the Camino trail is divided into 3 parts: BODY, MIND, and SOUL; a third of the total kilometres allotted to each part. It is said the Camino will test a pilgrim on each aspect until lessons are learned.

CHAPTER 1

Geese

DAY 1 October 13, 2012

(Sudbury, Ontario to Paris, France)

Geese flew into the engine. That's what really happened. I thought I had planned for everything. It's not like I hadn't had years to get organized, but for whatever reason, I didn't plan for Canada geese. And so... geese flew into the airplane engine, which is how my pilgrimage started.

I'm supposed to be flying to France today to start a Camino. I have healing to do. I have karma to bust up. I need a fresh start. So what I think will hammer it home the best for me is to take a nice... long... walk.

I met a pilgrim once who had hiked the Compostela de Santiago. She placed a stone into my hand and wished me a buen Camino. This happened during the darkest and lowest point in my life, and the words have since echoed in my head. *What did she mean?* For years, that stone kept turning up again and again like a silent taunt, until I agreed to do the walk. I acquiesced because it couldn't be any worse than chemotherapy, and by now the stone's calling had gotten me curious.

So 5 years and 11 months after my diagnosis, I'm packed, ready, and on my way. The Compostela trail starts in St. Jean Pied de Port, France, crosses the Pyrenees Mountains, and runs through the length of Spain for 800 km into the third holiest place in Christendom, called Santiago. Santiago is said to be the burial place of the Apostle St. James. I've timed my travels to coincide with the end of my breast cancer treatment. On October 15, 2007, I finished chemotherapy and radiation, and on that same day in 2012, I will be at the trailhead to start my pilgrimage, otherwise known as "Camino" or "The Way". A month after that, I will no longer be required to take my daily dose of Tamoxifen and I plan to throw my bottle of pills into the sea at Finisterre, or somewhere I deem worthy when the time comes. The last ten years have been a period of chaos, and I just need to put a lid on all of it. A lid labelled DISASTER.

My mind and my past need reconciling. I will have lots of time to be alone with my thoughts. I'm calling it my "Gratitude Pilgrimage", to say thank you for letting me live. And I mean it; I'm entirely grateful. I think, symbolically, if I can manage to do a pilgrimage, I must be well. I guess it wouldn't hurt to keep my heart and mind open either.

Strangely enough, I've asked my former off-and-on love interest, Grizzly, to drive me to the airport this morning. I supposed it might as well be him as a form of closure. The chemistry is crazy and it's hard to resist him, but I don't want to start my Camino longing for someone and something that will never be. The healing for everything in my life starts today. Grizzly arrives early and cooks me a breakfast of fresh farm eggs, as if nothing in the world is going on. He could have spent last night with me, but we both know it's over. He has bought me a Gortex jacket for my trip to keep me dry, and feeds me as a parting gift. It is our last meal together.

I guess it could have been worse. We hold hands all the way to the airport in near-silence. There is nothing left to say. There's no bridge big enough to narrow the gap. He wants his freedom and I want a partner. I've waited years for him to come around but the bottom line is he doesn't want me *enough*. And it hurts.

I smoke a wistful cigarette before I board the plane. I've slipped back into my old ways since I ran my first full marathon in July. Just wanting "to be bad a bit", has been my excuse for a while but the pull to smoke is as powerful now as the day I quit 6 years ago. It is a good cigarette, though I'm hopeful it will be my last. I board the plane after a tearful goodbye to Grizzly. While he drives away, I hold my head up high... It's the only thing you can do when you're entering a phase of prolonged celibacy.

And I'm off.

At what feels like warp speed, our plane hits a flock of Canada geese. For a second I think we have been shot down. Slaughtered bits are hitting and arcing off the plane with a cacophony of sound that is not all reassuring. I feel horrified for the geese, but I can only assume this is going to be an inconvenient delay. Back to the airport we trot one by one like good children and await our fate. The airline used different wording but we're told essentially our plane has been destroyed just enough for discontinued use at this time. A mechanic from Toronto will be flown (yada, yada) into Sudbury for repairs. I believe this is aviation speak for heaven only knows when the next flight will be. Does this kind of thing happen very often? TO ANYONE? This has been an outstanding morning so far. I only have something in the neighbourhood of 3 flights, 2 buses, and 3 or 4 trains to catch back-to-back.

Grateful to be ALIVE?

Sure!

Because I would have felt BLOODY WELL CHEATED if I'd died on day one!

I have another cigarette. So much for my latest resolution which lasted all of 45 minutes. I speak liberally here, but I feel strongly that break-ups and near death experiences (resulting from geese) require fortification. It is during fortification that I meet Marion. She is a tall, pretty, blond woman who is also smitten with the joy of smoking. Her carry-on is packed full--only with cigarettes. Giant Ziploc bags full of e-cigarettes, cartons of real cigarettes, and Nicorette gums. I ask her where she might be headed that she should supply herself with such a cornucopia.

We chat for a time and it turns out she is a 6-year cancer survivor. The irony of us both smoking our faces off is not lost on me. Her struggle with cancer has been a wicked one and I wonder if she is still on borrowed time. I'm not feeling glass-half-full at the moment. I philosophize to myself how the minute we're born, we're living on borrowed time. And so, we smoke, like it's all reasonable. What's reasonable is that we didn't just crash to our deaths because of Canada geese.

I see my friend George. He is my friend Pam's husband, and they are meeting in Vancouver for their 25 wedding anniversary. Really! How is 25 years even possible? My thoughts drift. My relationships span anywhere from 5 minutes to 7 years; including a turbulent marriage somewhere in there.

Have I learned nothing in 40 years? As far as I'm concerned, cigarettes lead to a more satisfying death than being saddled with the wrong chap.

The delay is similar to a root canal, but I get to Toronto in enough time to learn that my 2-hour window is chastened by the fact that all of the computers are down. I race through the airport with my backpack and heavy purse to find the right line. It can't produce tickets anyhow. I'm sweating and my bones are creaking under a weight that would make Navy Seals flinch. Well, maybe a baby seal. I've gone roughly 400 meters and I want to roll over and expose my belly.

I board the plane with 5 minutes to spare and am that asshole who walks onto the plane last, that everyone glares at, as if I'm the sole cause for the world's problems. I congratulate myself for being on this plane at all.

The next seven hours is only enjoyable because I've shed my backpack. I have the middle seat between two guys, one of whom has a lot to say. I feel like a squished éclair and force fed like a prized hog with our meals coming consecutively over what seems to be a 20 minutes span. It's going to take the jaws of life to get me out of this seat.

I leave a smelly, waxy muffin on the tray, mocking, "How can they serve this in France?"

In Paris, they have lost my backpack, and the general suspicion is that it has taken a short voyage over to Dubai.

CHAPTER 2

Travel Prison

DAY 2 October 14

(Paris to Biarritz)

The manual tickets got the wrong airport code. I have no choice but to leave the airport without my backpack and find the bus to ORLY airport. Yes, the hour-and-a-half-away airport. How did I not know this? Apparently, I'm in CHARLES DE GAULLE airport. I glance down at myself with the cold realization that I may be climbing the Pyrenees with 5 pieces of gum, 2 cigarettes, a pair of sunglasses, and my journal. I just went from being overly prepared (or at least overly weighted) to nada in seconds.

    Strangely, I feel no anxiety whatsoever. The close call earlier with the geese and this mounting fatigue, have me in a fairly decent place. I calculate that my hour-and-a-half bus ride should arrive at the ORLY airport, just as my next flight slowly departs.

Vive la France!

Buen Camino.

Shit happens.

Oh, what I wouldn't do for that smelly, waxy muffin.

I've had to make nice with the AIR FRANCE Lost Luggage department a few times today. Now I'm meeting with Christina, my last hope. She's telling me in a nasally French accent that it could be anywhere from a couple of days to two weeks to get my bag returned to me. "What airport is closest to my home in Canada to which they would send my bag?" I wilt. It only took me 4 years to get my equipment bought and paid for. She reassures me, "But Heather, you can buy *anything at all* in France. Do you have VISA?" I nod numbly.

I walk in the pouring rain to a nearby hotel and empty my wallet to pay for a room. No worries though: I've been giving a free bendy plastic toothbrush. I'm so hungry I'm considering eating the toothpaste, and it's not long before I find myself at the bar eating all of the free peanuts and washing them down with a tall lager. When Monsieur Concierge announces that my luggage will be here at 4:45 pm tomorrow, I can only nod in affirmation because I just can't muster up my fake smile. Smiling requires facial muscles, and mine are on strike at the moment after having been on standby for over 33 hours.

Sleep is elusive when you travel, isn't it? Why can't I sleep?

Just rest your body, Heather. Lie down and stop moving.

Never mind the rain, my mood is dampened at the realization that I won't be starting my Camino on October 15; this date is significant for me! Even if I get my bag tomorrow, I still won't be in the right town yet. I have to get myself to St. Jean Pied de Port and hope to God the Camino passport office is still open. That, and it seems foolhardy to cross the Pyrenees at night. I'm thinking I should wait until October 16 to commence. Now, what to do for the next 24 hours in limbo?

French television holds my attention for about 10 minutes. I take a bubble bath and wash my undergarments in the tub with my t-shirt and socks. With all of my undergarments wet, I go to a beautiful French restaurant essentially naked. I walk in with my chin up and shoulders back, wearing electric blue long underwear and my running jacket with nothing on underneath.

I recognize basically nada, zip, zero at the starter buffet, and instead settle in with a glass of fabulous Red Navarra. Or, I should say, *le vin rouge*. Dinner choices are daunting. Let's see, do I want mouth-watering veal kidneys, beef tartare, sautéed cuttlefish, gambas a la plancha... That last one sounds familiar. Relief: the special is an encrusted salmon with Hollandaise sauce, potatoes, and blood sausage. Guess whose luck is turning around! Salmon it is- hold the blood.

I finish up with an after-dinner coffee, and the waitress brings me an espresso. It's so phenomenal that I feel misty eyed. Full-bodied flavour alright. Now can I have a 32 ounce cup of that? Canada is all about hydration. A litre, give or take, of Tim Horton's coffee before lunch is simply our culture. I surmise that the French must all be very, very thirsty.

CHAPTER 3

Buses and Trains

DAY 3 October 15

(Biarritz to St. Jean Pied de Port)

Yawn. *Stretch.* Mother of God! The first day of my supposed Camino and I wake up at 11:00am; 13 hours after my head hit the pillow. I scramble out into the day and fall into the housekeeper's cart, which is directly outside my door. I guess I'm the last guest to leave. I look awful but I feel fantastic. I'm donning all of my damp clothing after hopelessly trying to attach my socks to the end of the hairdryer in an attempt to dry them. Note: this is not recommended. The hair dryer's plastic nozzle melted like wax and the socks remained… *wettish*.

Damp, but ready for the day, I have a mere 6 hours to wait for my luggage. I'm trying to check-out but I guess I look so pitiful that the restaurant owner tells me they're closed for breakfast.

"Oh! But it's *you* that has lost her luggage!"

He breathes out his words expressively in a way that only the French can. He offers me anything I want. I resist saying a 32 ounce coffee. I eat everything put before me with relish. "Ah yes. Heated milk with my café? But of course!" I could get used to this kind of service. I've been to only one place in France so far. And so far, it's my favourite place. It's the Amary's International Hotel in the Industrial part of Biarritz which happens to be 300 meters from the airport.

It's about 16 degrees and sunny, and I'm wearing three damp jackets. At least I have my sunglasses! Only 4 more hours until I get my luggage. I still have to take a bus to the train station. There is a train to Bayonne, then another to St. Jean Pied de Port arriving at 8:07pm. The passport office will most certainly be closed; but at least I'm inching myself in the right direction.

To kill time, my mind is chattering to me in run-on sentences and scattered thoughts. I'm thinking about how the French are highly efficient and that the people have been so nice and polite and helpful, but also how nothing is efficient at all without your baggage.

I'm in travel prison!!

French bathrooms smell delicious. I swear they are cleaned with Coco Chanel. I'm clearly fatigued and losing my mind, but I am tempted to dip my hands into the cleaning solution and splash about. The help looks at me suspiciously as I lean over to sniff. 3 hours and 25 minutes to go. On the home stretch now. Boredom has left me outright strange.

Surprise, surprise! I discover yet another French bar. Bars are the only thing I'm really good at finding. Heineken is my chosen antidote for today's blisteringly long wait. I anticipate a staggering response to the weight of my yet-to-be-seen backpack and the beer buzz. One bus and two trains until I can finally *start*. Once a critic of the "stupid people" on *The Amazing Race*, I now completely empathize with their travel setbacks. I've been traffic-watching for hours, and I've noticed that the taxi cabs are all Mercedes. The masses drive Peugeot and Audi. "How lovely," I mutter to myself. In Sudbury, the masses drive trucks and Honda Civics. I'm wondering if *anyone* in Europe drives a Honda.

As forecasted, my blessed pack comes careening around the luggage belt, and my hand goes instinctively over my heart, as if I'm seeing a loved one. I can barely lift it and I have to fight to get it on my back. Some bastard has added things. I make my way to line C to catch the bus to the train station. I don't dare start thinking I'm on my way yet. *Why is this so hard already?*

The weight of my backpack concerns me; my right hip feels like it may actually dislocate. I adjust this strap and that strap and it doesn't improve, so it can only be that I have an undiagnosed condition of hip dysplasia; like over-bred retrievers. I would love another Heineken… for the pain.

I've deduced my first nugget of Camino wisdom today: I should not travel alone. Period. Jet-lagged right down to my toenails and not really "plugged in" shall we say, I pull my biggest bonehead move yet. I'm waiting and waiting for my train to arrive. I get my ticket and sit on the closest bench outside. I light a smoke and wait some more. A train arrives on the other side of the tracks, and as it's about to pull away, it daftly occurs to me that I'm not exactly sure *which side* my train is arriving on. That could be *my* train! I run like hell to catch the train like a calf trying to avoid a roping. All helter-skelter, I board; breathless, sweaty, and playing it cool like I'd timed it this way.

As it turns out, the French countryside is breathtaking. The train rolls over the tracks passing lush green hills and forest until we reach the town of Bayonne. I get off the train to wait for the next one and notice that there are four tracks this time. Each track has trains going in different directions. It's an underground maze to find where I'm supposed to be waiting. I figure the best thing to do is to do is ask the best looking fellow I can find to show me the way.

In St. Jean Pied de Port I meet Amiry from Finland. We walk together to the pilgrim office, which happens to be open until 10:00 pm! It's my second miracle today. I look around at the other pilgrims and note my backpack is at least double in size to everyone else's. I get called crazy twice tonight as they estimate my bag to be at least 15 kg. One seasoned traveller is carrying a mere 5 kg. I feel desperate.

What could I possibly discard? Should I shame myself at the albergue and spread everything out like a Moroccan bazaar? I am so fucked for the Pyrenees.

We dine together as albergue mates: a mix of Finn (Amiry), Australian (Nadine), English, Irish, Spanish, and Italian (Maximus). Albergues, or refugios, as they are sometimes called, are hostels for pilgrims. We are told by the hospitalero that we have to sleep in until 7:00 am, and no shoes are to be worn in the house. This albergue keeper is no nonsense. She shows us laminated pictures of shoes with a red line through them. Gotcha. Right. We get it. Tomorrow, I need to find a bookstore.

I need a guide book. I *thought* there would be one to buy at the pilgrim office, because that would be a GOOD THING TO SELL TO PILGRIMS! *NO?* I don't have a map, or a list of town names or distances between albergues, except a scrap of paper where I jotted down a tentative itinerary self-titled *Compostela in 30 days*. I am grossly unprepared in every way. I'm winging it, and stupid doesn't even begin to describe how I'm feeling right now. *I bet the other pilgrim have maps… I shall boldly follow them.*

As we reach the albergue, Francesco says, "Was that large statue there before? What is it?" I reply, "A blow up doll I think". Amiry gasps. "Heather! That's the Angel of Peace!" "Oooh," I breathe with downcast eyes. We are surrounded by so much garish adornment right now that I really couldn't have known. I turn in.

For now I think it's best I zip my pie-hole.

CHAPTER 4

I'm Sure It's Fine

DAY 4 October 16

(St. Jean Pied de Port to St. Jean Pied de Port)

The morning's shower is an ice cold, freezing-ass shower. I've had Canadian polar dips warmer than this. I barely get my bits. Later, there is an INTERVENTION regarding my backpack. I'm surrounded by concerned pilgrims. "You must NOT cross the Pyrenees this way!" They have weighed my pack in at 23 kg. "Impossible!" I shriek. I'm beaten at my own hand and I know it. I shuffle off to the nearest post office; mostly because that's the fastest pace I can go. This is where I bravely chose to spread out my Moroccan bazaar of personal belongings; all over the post office floor. I am able to shed a glorious 5.5kg and I feel like it's a champion effort. Beautiful French women peer down their noses initially with curiosity, then an obvious hint of disgust after an hour and a half. The whole situation costs me €50.

Next on the agenda is trying to find a guidebook. I find three bookstores and wouldn't you know it, not one of them has anything in English. Well, I'm sure it's fine to hike 800 km without a map.

By now, I am the last pilgrim to leave St. Jean Pied de Port. It's 11:00 am. If I'd HAD a guide book I would have learned that it is best to leave at 7:00 am to cross the Pyrenees.

About half an hour into the whole shebang, it starts to pour, creating a muggy brew in the air. I hate my backpack passionately and I'm at least 4 hours behind everyone else. I may have bitten off more than I can chew.

About an hour on the road, I take out my camera, and with the precision of a sharpshooter I take my first photo. *'This camera does not take this card'* flashes across the screen. Ahhhhh! You have got to be kidding me! So, I guess no Compostela photos. I continue. At hour 2, I'm still looking for a Camino sign. It's my first day on the trail and I'm clueless as to the frequency of signs for this. I stop and ask for directions in such broken 4th grade French that I'm giggling. What's worse is I learn that this mountain I've just spent the last two hours hiking up is the *wrong* mountain!

13:30 pm. At a bar, I talk a customer and his wife into a ride back to St. Jean Pied de Port. They agree to do it, however, they would like to go home and have lunch first. But of course! I've got nothing but time. As natural as breathing, I order a beer and something to eat in order to pass the time. Waiting patiently for things is becoming a refined gift in me. I think it may very well be my only gift. Who am I kidding? I am the WORST pilgrim on this entire *planet*. Hold on a second: while all those other suckers are toiling up the *real* Pyrenees, I'm over here (but where?) drinking a beer and boning up on my French. *It's all learning, Heather.*

Is it too late in the day to get over the Pyrenees to the town of Ronconcevelles? It's a gruelling 7-8 hour hike of Hell, I'm told. Sunset is at 7:00 pm. I'm considering this like it's still an option. I can't even find my way around in broad daylight. It took me days to get myself to the gate and now I have to go back to the gate.

The Compostela has been the Compostela for a thousand years, but I don't even know if that's true without a bleepin' guidebook. My point is, in all that time, has *anyone* ever hiked 2 hours in the wrong direction on DAY *fucking* ONE?! I've lost 4 days now. I wonder about Finisterre. Any number of calamities undoubtedly still await me; after all it's me we're talking about: the *world's worst pilgrim*. At the rate I'm going, I may never reach

Santiago. "Another beer, por favor. Un autre Boisson, merci." I don't even know what I'm saying; I'm mixing two languages together that I don't even speak. Clearly, I should have gone on to Dubai with my bag.

ESTERENCUBY. This is where I am. I have a guy in the bar write down the name of the town for me as the "nom de ville, ici". The lady behind the bar pulls out a large map and shows me where we are. I ask her to show me where St. Jean is on the map in relation to *here*. With one finger on ESTERENCUBY she then points to a spot on the countertop that is about 4 inches entirely off the map.

I am the laughing stock of France right now. I'm for sure the laughing stock of the bar… in ESTERENCUBY. Je suis très stupide, alors fatigué, alors… etc. I self-deprecate. The joy of drinking beer in ESTERENCUBY is not intolerable seeing as it was only this week that I had nearly met my maker via Canada Geese.

Let's not be hasty. Enjoy the moment. Oh look! Le soleil. Sigh. There should be an award or booby prize for the worst traveller. Like the Stanley Cup. If I only had room in my backpack.

The scallop shell, commonly found on the shores of Galicia is the official symbol of the Compostela de Santiago. The shell, along with yellow arrows, is used to denote signage along the trail to help guide pilgrims. That's what I hear anyway. Not because I have actually laid eyes on a sign, shell, arrow, or smoke signals of any kind indicating The Way of St. James. It has been said that pilgrims often take to wearing a shell attached to their backpacks to prove they are travellers along the Way. This is helpful, I imagine, when pilgrims get lost so that locals can easily identify us and hopefully point us in the right direction. Perhaps if I had been wearing a shell earlier, I may have manifested directional support, because clearly hauling a gigantic backpack did not.

I haven't bought the standard pilgrim shell yet for a couple of reasons. First, it weighs in like gold. Second, I haven't earned one. I haven't actually taken a step on the real bonafide trail. The acquisition of a pilgrim shell has fallen completely off my list of priorities while my spirit plummets 50 feet underground. Well, looky there! Le bonhomme de ESTERENCUBY with his wife, his sister, and her husband have come back to collect me. It is akin to a mirage because I had only half vested hope that this sweet Samaritan would return.

Their story is this.

I learn that le bonhomme's family has just arrived, for one day only, after a 400 mile journey to get here. Guess how these fine folks get to spend it? We all pile into something smaller than a smart car, with my abomination of a pack lying across our laps. Honestly, I have no words for how sheepish I feel.

To lessen my personal shame, I ask in Frenglish whether there is anywhere else I can go lick my wounds just outside of the city - I am too embarrassed to go back to St. Jean Pied de Port. "It is possible", they tell me with understanding smiles. There happens to be an albergue 5 km out from the city. Really? It's 3:30 pm. I've bravely gone 8 km up the wrong mountain, only to go back 3 km so that I can proudly say I've traversed a mighty 5 km in the wrong direction of the sacred St. James trail.

I don't care. I'm counting it.

It's sunny and I'm overlooking the most beautiful valley I've ever seen, so far. At this point, the industrial district of Biarritz would have pleased me just as well. Seeing as my day has ended early, I grab another beer and stare at the valley. Because I'm an overachiever, that's why!

I'm not sure exactly why I'm indulging in all of this alcohol. I never drank at all in my 20's and drank very little in my 30's. In recent years, I've learned to lighten up a bit and have more of a good time - since I can. Since I'm alive and such. Anyway, I'm on holiday, if that's what you want call all of this nonsense.

The beer is Akerbeltz "Biere Brasse au pays Basque", a local beer after all. There is a ram on the label. How much ram is in it? I can't really say. It seems authentic enough for me because I've seen quite a few rams around these parts.

"La terre magnifique" is the last statement I've made to a real live person, and I fear that my personality, along with my IQ, is being lost in translation. My only companion now is a *gris chat*. It is incredible how much shitty, broken French slang I'm using. Not that the cat understands me. Like most cats, this one is somewhat devoted, while infuriatingly elusive; sort of like my last love conquest.

I'M SURE IT'S FINE

This albergue is completely empty. Of course it is! What idiot can't walk 5km on the first day! I marvel that the albergue has stayed in business at all. Surprisingly, supper does end up being lively, as the albergue has filled up with other pilgrims. I wonder what in God's green earth happened to them that they could only walk 5 km today?

Everyone I've met is worried about me.

"Heather, do you have a cell phone?"

"Non."

"A map?"

"Non."

"A guidebook of some kind?"

"Non."

"How much does that pack of yours weigh anyhow?"

I shrug.

We talk until late, and turn in. I shower with the novelty of hot water, which is reward enough for this day. Yup! Being a pilgrim sure is hot and dusty work! I have a room to myself and my clothes have exploded everywhere in decoration in an effort to dry them. There had better not be an inspection 'cause this is a wrap.' Bonne nuit!

CHAPTER 5

Crossing the Pyrenees

DAY 5 OCT 17

(St. Jean Pied de Port to somewhere not called St. Jean Pied de Port)

I should *really* start this Camino today! I didn't sleep much last night due to a wind/rain storm that sounded like a level 5 hurricane. Doors banged and the walls shuttered in a way that made me wonder if we would all be huffed and puffed en masse into the valley.

It was the storm of a lifetime. It felt like the walls were going to tear apart. Never have I heard wind force of that nature, and I worried that I would not be able to start the Camino because of it. I swore to myself (while in the safety of my bed) that if I had to do the Camino in a bloody canoe, I would. No more obstacles! Adapt. Overcome.

By morning, the rain has subsided, but the wind has me unbalanced. An otherworldly sunrise beholds the land and valley below, which I take foolishly as a good omen.

I get started at 8:22 am. Not bad! The progress is slow but steady, and completely vertical for the entire day. The scenery is magnificent, but for the first time on my trip, I am terrified. I'm making only about 2 km/hour for the first 3 hours due to the wind. A few times, it takes me nearly 30 minutes to go roughly 400 meters. I have to stop and plant my hiking poles into the earth, knees bent and trying my damnedest to stay upright. There is a head wind and side wind working against me. Three times I am blown unceremoniously off my feet flying 6-8 feet. I have never been so out of control because of the elements, and there is no shelter anywhere. I'm like a sheet of paper blowing in the wind. If it weren't for my hiking poles, I would probably blow off into the Pyrenees and no one would even know.

Then, it occurs to me that nobody would know to come looking for me for 6 weeks or so. I'm off the map. No cellphone, no internet. Nothing. I could simply blow away and vanish without a trace. The physical feeling I am experiencing might be similar to wading through waist-high mud, or perhaps a space-walk; not that I've tried either of those things. Each step forced and planted, and there is nothing natural or progressive about it. It is terrifying for me. This isn't an issue of fitness or mental strength; it is simply a near impossibility to go forward in these conditions. I have no idea if the winds are like this year-round (and the pilgrims I speak with later tell me they've never experienced anything like it). I understand now on an instinctual level how some pilgrims have lost their lives on this trail. I'm sweating fear.

By either grit or stupidity, I end up achieving approximately 35 km today. I guess that is what adrenaline does for you. I hiked mostly alone but met some interesting characters later on when the winds died down and it was possible to speak to one another. My new friends are Benjamin and Jae Min from South Korea, Roberto from Italy, and Thomas from Germany, who dined with me last night.

Jae Min from South Korea looks uncannily like Kim Jong-Un, the leader of North Korea. I did a double take when I first saw him, and he understood immediately. "I know. I look a great deal like him. It is unfortunate that I can't change my face." I laugh with him and suggest he never take a career in politics no matter what his inclination or aptitude. I'm picturing comedians on late night television doing skits, newly minted comic books, never mind the editorial page of every newspaper on the planet. I foresee political backlash, harassment in airports, and a WW3 outbreak. Jae Min is a sweet and honourable young man. Please don't judge him by his face.

Benjamin has a lot of questions for me regarding whether I think Asian men are good looking. Why don't more white women date Asian men? Do I think he is handsome? Have I ever dated an Asian man? Oh my. "Um, well I have never dated an Asian man but I thought the new lead singer for Journey looked pretty good in white jeans." I try to explain to him how it's not necessarily an aversion to Asian men, it's possibly a supply issue. I haven't met too many, having lived most of my life in redneck territory. I describe my type as, "mainly hairy men that are kind of thicker." Wow. Just saying that out loud makes me want to re-evaluate my entire dating history.

Roncesvalles feels strange to me and I hesitate to stay there. Roberto urges me to walk on, so I do. I can't explain what I am feeling exactly but the atmosphere is loud and silly with arriving pilgrims. It's probably just their happiness for having survived the mountains, but I am seeking peaceful surroundings tonight. I'm sensitive to energy; I need to refuel and reflect, and I just don't think I'm going to get that here. I guess I'm supposed to walk a little more today, for whatever reason, so I might as well get on with it.

We walk the streets of a Spanish town whose name I can't recall, sipping a beautiful 2007 Spanish wine from Dixie cups. I suspect my journal will have zero historical facts in it without a guide book, and it could very well be page after page of daily minutia with a side dish of emotional caterwauling.

Stretched out in our rooms, we exchange e-mail addresses (with the girl who doesn't have internet back home). I don't know if I will see any of these people again, and yet though our ages span, we have become kindred spirits. I feel grateful, happy, and peaceful. It was the right thing to walk on, after all.

It is very cold tonight. I sleep poorly but restfully in my own private room. I'm in a beautiful old Spanish house, but it is not heated. My clothes are wet and dirty, but the blankets are warm. I just need to toughen up.

These are first world problems. I'm sore from the day so I take 2 Ibuprofen and a Benadryl tablet to help me sleep. I toss myself into a straight jacket made of blankets.

CHAPTER 6

Duct Tape

DAY 6 October 18

(Somewhere to somewhere else)

I awake refreshed but chilled by the stark morning air. I pack quickly and have breakfast with Thomas, my new delightfully gay friend. He is truly sensational in many regards. He is wise, positive, and always smiling; he's a pleasant influence for anyone to be around. We start to hike together in the dark, just before 8:00 am. My pace is slow and we are once again climbing upward. I tell him to go on and he does.

I'm not sure how far I will make it today. My muscles are screaming and my feet are ruined. My heels peeled off overnight, so I've applied an over-the-counter product called New Skin and secured duct tape over top. Not exactly doctor recommended. New blisters are forming under my heels and my toenails are loose. I'm questioning these $300 hiking boots I deemed essential; they are undoubtedly too small for me now, under the weight of my backpack.

I enter a forest and hike for hours alone. I prefer it this way. I'm smiling and walking at a snail's pace: about 3.5km per hour. That's disappointing to calculate, but I know I can keep going until I get to somewhere. I come across a memoriam for a Japanese man who lost his life on the Camino. The plaque doesn't divulge how he died and my mind imagines an assortment of possible untimely deaths. I find myself choked up, and shed a few silent tears. I have nothing to leave, so I pour some of my juice over the rocks and branches others have left to mark the spot. I take a swig of juice myself and say, "Buen Camino, pilgrim". *Time to go, Heather.* I wander and wander, wondering if I'm even on the right trail. I stop to void and realize my best parts are over brambles and I am being pricked to Betsy. *There is a whole entire forest to pick from Heather and you picked the brambley section?* My intuition is not so finely tuned today.

After a few hours, my feet are complaining. I'm almost ready to give it a go barefoot when I come across a bull in my path. I freeze like a deer. I have only my box of juice and my camera at the ready. We stare at one another in a show down. "What should I do?" I ask the Bull. I tell him "*GO AWAY!*" in my toughest voice. He steps forward. "Do you want some juice? Your picture? Some KitKat?"

I know… I pull out my flashlight and advance. The moment I switch it on, the Bull spooks and runs off willy nilly.

Yeah, that's right! Fear me, nature's children.

The rest of the way is dangerously down, down, down with loose rocks and mud. I can't believe I'm going to say this, but I think I prefer going up. I saunter into the next town, limping, and take a break.

I see Thomas and Roberto, and hug them both. I'm so happy to see my new friends. I love hiking alone, but when I'm done, I want to drink beer and talk, and thus this recluse becomes a socialite.

Naturally, we head to the bar. There doesn't seem to be in the Western world sense, any restaurants. They are all bars that serve food. I haven't been to a real bar in about 20 years, but now it's a daily event on the Camino. We find an Alburgue afterwards and then do our laundry. It's nice enough to hang our laundry ourside. No rain or so much as a cloud in the sky. We decide we should picnic; and procure ourselves with cheese, baguettes, pate, beer and prosciutto (jamon) then head for the ambling riverside. We dine like Kings and Queens must; meditate and write in our journals. Today is my favourite day so far.

DUCT TAPE

When we return my clean laundry has blown itself all over the muddy yard. Roberto says "Heather, you should see this, come". I see the problem and tuck my muddy white underwear into my jacket slightly embarrassed. Later on, we cook dinner together where we are staying. Thomas and I make salad and leave Roberto the Italian to the spaghetti sauce. A Spaniard we've dubbed 'the mushroom man' has found local fungi and we add it to the sauce. It's delicious so I ask you "Why not eat strange mushrooms from a stranger"? We empty bottles of Spanish wine and smoke French cigarettes in the rain. Somehow, with bits and pieces of French, English, and Spanish we are able to communicate some laughs. The Pyronees, now seems like a bad dream I once had.

Thomas started his Camino the old traditional way; from his home town, which happens to be Munich, Germany. Sam, who is 19 years old from Boston, started in the middle of the trail, then thought better of it and went back to Roncesvalles. The Spaniard, Aurie has until Christmas to travel and another pilgrim wants to get to Finisterre. We all want to get to Finisterre. We are limping and sore, but determined. I put my earplugs in tonight because the Alburgue is a large common room with about 40 co-ed beds. My feet throb all night and I toss and turn, listening to the dampened sounds of pilgrims snoring.

CHAPTER 7

Ghost Towns

DAY 7 October 19 - 7:00 am

(Somewhere else to Pamplona)

I pack up and hit the road when it's still dark outside. Nothing is open. I learn that the next town is 1.5 hours away and that there will be coffee and breakfast there. I've never had to wait more than 10 minutes to drink coffee once my eyelids blink open! How will I make it? I take a sip of tepid water and step out into the rain. The goal today is to get to Pamplona. It will be Friday night and pretty happening from what I understand. My heels are still duct taped, so I should be able to get there eventually. Roberto, Thomas and I walk together as 3 compadres/amigos/friends to the next town, where we discover there really is no coffee because nothing at all is open. Roberto sweetly informs me the distance to the next town where there is sure to be coffee for me, and then the distance to the next town, and then yes, the next. At this point, I'm simply losing my will to live. At 3:00 pm, we find a bar that is actually open and I order both a coffee and a beer with my breakfast.

Earlier, we had passed through several towns with breathtaking Basque architecture, but there was not a single soul to be found. These were eerily quiet ghost towns. It was as though we were on a Hollywood film set and the show would begin at any moment. But nothing ever did. What was the reason for this? Was it due to an economic downturn? How can entire towns be emptied out? I had never seen this anywhere before now. We munched on jambon chips along the way; the crunch of our chips and the sound of our steps being the only sounds for miles around. It was all very surreal.

Roberto and I are the slow, injured pilgrims; his knee and my… well, everything. My left leg is swollen from my knee to my toes and it is quite unrecognizable. Thomas, strides ahead and soon his shrinking image is out of sight. He makes walking look effortless. I suppress my envy by swallowing more flavoured ham chips. Why don't they just sell bags of ham?

Walking should really be easier. After all, humans *are* bipedal. It is in our very nature to walk; not drive, not fly, not ride horses or whatever the going modality is from century to century. If we were meant to have wheels, we would have grown some by now. Today, it has become nearly obsolete to walk anywhere; it's much too time intensive. We are a society that values the mind and every possible time-saving apparatus. We strive to utilize our down time and multitask the shit out of everything to the point that walking has lost its practical appeal. To walk towards enlightenment would be unthinkable as a career choice; because in this day and age you would up and starve to death. Centuries ago, most people were long dead by the age of 67. The cliché phrase 'out of balance' is, frankly, an epidemic.

If you think about it, we should walk more often for a whole host of reasons! For example, it is an activity that is free of charge, in an era of blossoming consumer debt. We can't afford *not* to walk. Consider also that there is no global, ecological, or economic impact. It is not offensive politically or religiously to go out walking and the health benefits are innumerable. It gently decompresses the frazzled human brain instead of having to pay thousands of dollars for a shrink. All the while giving you boundless energy, clearing up your skin, sleeping better and generally speaking, you just feel better after you do it.

Never once did my mother ever say to me, "Don't you even *think* about going outside and walking. I forbid it!" Nope, we spent our childhoods walking, running, climbing, and scraping up our shins by falling off our bicycles. We grew up hardy and lean and as far as I can tell, it has served us well. Back then there wasn't any Playstation, or any Insta-Face Twitter bleeping going on because there were no laptops yet. Computers were just becoming available to the general public. We had floppy disks and car phones. We were, of course, that family who bought a Betamax VCR, when everyone else in the solar system bought VHS. There were limits on television time, and nothing on the tube required parental supervision. It was a simpler time. It was awesome!

Long before this, Sages and Sufi alike wandered the earth to navigate the muddy labyrinth of the mind, in search of enlightenment. They were striving to transcend pain and suffering to the point that the universe apparently took pity and opened itself up by pouring down all of its knowledge upon them. It was revered. It was a calling. It was work. I'm not entirely sure what they ate or who paid for it. I liken it to gap years for older men. For sure, somebody helped these guys!

To me, walking is kind of like painting a room: you can't easily visualize your accomplishment until completion. I just looked over my shoulder and saw the majestic Pyrenees behind me. It was truly worth the agony.

Midday at the bar, Roberto and I run into Thomas who is already piss drunk off his gizzard. He proclaims he has had about 10 cigarettes and 5 beers; gloating as if he's just won the Nobel Peace Prize. He says he hiked quite fast but wanted to wait for us. He is dry and smiling.

I, on the other hand, am soaked to my spleen, freezing and covered in disgusting viscous mud. I look like I've just returned from the Vietnam War. Thomas looks as though he has just finished a GQ magazine photo shoot and his shirt is still pressed. I try to hate him. Why is it that gay men stay so clean? We see Aurie, a fellow pilgrim, a.k.a. the mushroom man, wearing white pants of all things; white, corduroy pants. In this MUD AND RAIN?! He could not have surprised me more had he ridden into the bar on a unicorn.

There is a show about moose on television and I think wistfully of Canada. I grew up the youngest of three siblings and our parents were good to take us on many trips over the years. These included many a camping excursion with portages in the canoes, fishing, swimming in freshwater lakes, and camping across Canada to the West Coast. I remember the West Coast trip like it was yesterday because it happened to rain for 30 days straight and our tents never really dried completely. We were moist, muddy, and stinking the entire time, which is kind of how I'm feeling right this minute. I guess it's in my blood to be so … earthy.

Pamplona is about 5 km away and we eventually head out in that direction; after plying ourselves with agreeable sustenance. Thomas and Roberto are singing silly songs and playing some tiny musical instrument I've never seen before. It makes a *boing* sound, and when paired with sing-song, should really be aired with Mr. Roger's 'On Acid' Neighbourhood. I'm laughing my head off and I can't stop. They are behaving like good-natured little boys and the ridiculousness is good medicine.

The first refugio we come to is run by a German couple. They are full but let us use the bathroom. Hallelujah! Muchas gracias. It is these little things in life that mean so much.

We see Sam in the foyer because he is checked into this place for the night. We plan to meet up later on, but we never do.

All I want to do is shower, wash my clothes, and take these diabolical boots off. Not in that order. The albergue we choose is in the center of town and it's totally kickass. It has a futuristic decor and is only 3 months old. Not to mention it has hot water and a real washer and dryer that work.

I meet an Italian woman named Tercilla, who arrives holding her wrist. It's obvious that it's broken and I have to convince her to go to the hospital for an X-ray. She tells me it happened a day ago in one of the villages after she had slipped on mud. She wants to just wrap it and go on. Since I know zero Italian except the word spaghetti, I resort to hand signals, grave facial expressions, and a graver tone of voice to get my point across. The refugio owner agrees to take her for medical attention. It makes me think about how many people have died on the Camino. There have been quite a few markers along The Way. It's a lot to take in. The rest of us are here simply for the suffering. I'm finding that carrying the weight of our backpacks is punishment enough for our sins.

Once refreshed, we hit the town. Roberto would like to have a beer in every bar before dinner. This seems like a reasonable challenge. Most pilgrims do a layover in Pamplona and stay an extra day because it's so beautiful and exciting. The streets are lively and filled with people talking, drinking, and smoking. The atmosphere is a contrast to the miles of silence beforehand. When we are successfully lit, Thomas, Roberto, and I find an outstanding Spanish restaurant and leave the other pilgrims to cook in the refugio. It's 9:00 pm and I have no energy to cook tonight. We dine on shrimp and calamari, pork, red peppers, and potatoes, paired with a 2006 Spanish wine. It's such a lovely dinner I could cry for joy. Eating a good meal after a hard day of hiking is important not just for the stomach but for the weary soul. I simply love Pamplona.

The rain has stopped and we go out dancing till 1:30 am. The band is phenomenal. Their sound is a mix between Depeche Mode and U2, and they are touring throughout Europe. I grab their card for memory's sake. I get spun around and danced dizzy by handsome Spanish men. It is as glorious as it is harmless and *muy caliente*. We roll into our refugio with our keys and notice we are the last ones to arrive.

CHAPTER 8

Grit

```
DAY 8 October 20
Pamplona to Puenta La Reina
```

Strangely enough, I am the first to awaken. My feet and left leg roar with pain when they hit the floor. I will be walking on sheer grit today. I can't even walk normally. Daily foot care is the norm now, being a pilgrim, and it's a bloody surgery every night. I creep downstairs and pierce my blisters with a needle, dragging multiple threads through to keep things draining throughout the day. New blisters have formed under the old blisters and the whole mess is bruised and bloody. The backs of my heels peeled off days ago and are infected now. The other blisters are manageable, however, it's the swelling that is most worrisome to me. This is a boot problem, plain and simple… Or maybe it's a blood clot.

These are the same damn boots I used to hike over Bavarian and Austrian mountains last fall. They've been broken in! The difference I gather is that I carried only a day pack then and had my larger pack ferried onward to the next town. I suspect that the weight of the pack changes your foot size. Have my arches fallen completely? I'm not sure whether I can blame these boots for leg swelling; I suspect it will last for the duration of the trip. Long story short, I need new boots. These are garbage.

I leave the refugio at dark and start the day shifting my weight from one hip to the other in a steady limp. I simply cannot walk correctly. It's too painful. On to Puenta La Reina I go. It's a deluge of rain the entire way. My legs are soaked along with my footwear, and my backpack cover has slid up a bit drowning the bottom contents of my bag. I have added gallons to my freight. I'm only able to manage about 2 km /hr. A lot of pilgrims are passing me, but I'm not discouraged by this. I've resorted to wearing my sandals and strap my boots to the outside of my pack. What discourages me today is that I have had to watch every step I take and thus have had to forfeit the countryside view most of the day. The path is a river of mud, and my socks *squish* and *squish*.

There is really nowhere to go to the bathroom, so I find a tree and hope I am indeed the last pilgrim. I try singing in the rain to pass the time and find myself crying off and on. I'm exhausted and in agony. It's only the beginning of the Camino and it has seriously kicked my ass. I left my cigarettes in Pamplona, vowing piously to quit today. If I had any rolling papers right now, I would smoke my shoelace. I don't know what kind of miracle I'm expecting, but it isn't happening. It is cold and desolate out here, and I created this reality by coming here. I have no one to blame but myself, and I am trying to sit with that.

By the time I get to Puenta La Reina, it is completely dark and the rain hasn't stopped. I cannot feel my fingers or my hands. I am shivering so much that I can't open my wallet to pay at the albergue. I end up handing it over to some guy behind the counter, wherein he takes his required lot.

I splurge and get a private room. I can't deal with other people tonight. There is hot water, so I stand in the shower for as long as I can stand. My injuries are substantial and the edema has worsened. It's prudent that I should, from here on out, try to avoid gangrene. Thus, I make a plan to stay for 2 days in order to recuperate. It's okay. I accept it. Since tomorrow is Sunday, I can only assume everything is closed. This leaves me to find new boots on Monday and mail my other boots home. Another late start, but at least I will hopefully be able to continue on to Santiago.

I meet up with other pilgrims due to the ailing fact that I need food. They are encouraging. Helena from Switzerland and a chap from Portugal treat me to their tale of walking for three hours in the wrong direction and nearly freezing to death today. They will go on tomorrow, but tell me to rest and enjoy. Portugal says he may hang out in Santiago for a few days to see who arrives. I hope I make it, but it seems daunting to me. Finisterre seems even more remote now when I think of my earlier arrogant and lofty goal.

The Camino sure takes the ego out of you in a hurry. It's time for me to rest and regroup. Go on and let it rain. Perhaps Monday will be a better day for walking and for sun.

I give in and buy some cigarettes. The albergue has a beautiful veranda where I meet up with two guys from Finland who are stationed here to do electrical work at a nearby plant. We drink beer and smoke. They are entertaining and chatty which is good for me because an hour ago I was bawling my eyes out. The combination of Ibuprofen, beer, and good company has my spirits lifted to a near exultant height, leaving me wondering if I'm getting a mild case of the bipolar.

There have been so many obstacles and delays on this Camino that I have never, thankfully, encountered before. At some point, I need to analyze my money situation. My American Express card didn't work in France. I have to keep some hope that it will work in Spain. I did call them to let them know beforehand that I would be travelling. I still have Visa and euros galore but I will have to watch it. Less wine? Never!

I collapse into bed at 10:30 pm. I had planned to meet the Finlanders for another beer, saying I'll be back in 5 minutes. Instead, I laid down to stretch out for just a second and the next thing I know, it's morning. I will go ahead and apologize now, if that's alright, fellas.

CHAPTER 9

Boots

DAY 9 October 21

(Puenta La Reina)

I visit with pilgrims to say goodbye as they venture out into the rain. I know I likely won't see any of them again. One Aussie fellow left his wallet in Pamplona and is taking the bus back to the albergue to get it. Oh man, that's a real bummer. I run into a Canadian couple that I met on the trail yesterday and we get to talking about the winds from the first day. They said they were advised to go around the mountain instead of up and over it. They still found at times the wind gusts to be overwhelming. They were told about 5 times a year the winds from North Africa blow in, and that yesterday is was over 100km/hr winds. "Much too dangerous to go over the mountain." No shit, Sherlock! I obviously did not receive that classified Intel. So then, why have I had all of these near death experiences? The plane? The winds? All I can think about is *foot pain,* I muse at this point; if I was going die at a young age, I would have already been a goner. I'm still here, so suck it up, Princess!

I find a good table in the bar and put my feet up. I let the flies do what they want to my blisters. *Yes, that's it boys sop it all up.* Even though I'm dry, I'm freezing. Maybe, I have a fever. No period either now for a month and a half. Looks like I'm going through menopause again, which might explain some of the night sweats. Menopause has been an off and on thing for me since chemotherapy. I think it shrivelled my little ovaries. Well, it's beautiful luck, as far as I'm concerned. I would just as soon not have to deal with any womanly issues for a time. Maybe this explains some of my pathological fatigue. No problem, only 700+/- km to go.

An older gentleman approachs me speaking Dutch. We combine a few languages to make conversation. He has done the Camino 22 times from what I gather, unless something has been lost in translation. I don't mean this to come off as judgemental, but he looks about 100 years old and as sleek as Jabba the Hut. I can't get my jaw off the table. Is this truth or fiction? I'm a totally suck pilgrim. Fitness doesn't seem to be the main asset in doing the Camino. It's more than that. You have to want to do it more than it makes sense to do it.

I have time to write and reflect, so I do. There have been beautiful parts to the pilgrimage but I have been too lost in my misery to give them the appreciation and credit they deserve until now. I have eaten wild blackberries and plums from the forest, stepped over thousands of walnuts and a multitude of berries dotting the countryside that I cannot name or dare to try. I have eaten wild mushrooms, passed vineyards, farmland, and countless orchards in the rain. I have few photos because of the weather and my effort to protect the camera that doesn't belong to me (I found a memory card that works!). I noticed that every home has beautiful gardens that are lush and plentiful. I think of my garden back home. The one I plant every year and then don't tend to or water. *Do what you must plants; live or die.* I'm often surprised at how life... wants life.

I think about all the people who have helped me get to this point from back home: friends and family who are caretaking and managing my things while I'm away. I think of the little but really big things they have done and are doing as I sit here and eat local olives and pickles with my baguette of cheese and jamon. You know who you are and I thank you, wholeheartedly.

I'm taking another nap in my room of co-ed bunk beds when a pleasant and chatty man from France arrives. Enter Jean Lou. We decide to take a stroll into town in the spirit of recognisance regarding where the shoe store and post office are. This will save me time tomorrow morning. It becomes a project in itself, however, because places are not so well marked in this part of Spain. We have asked dozens of locals but no one has been able to help us find what we are looking for. How is it that if you're a local, you don't know where the only *zapatería* (shoe store) is? But in the end, it turns we've walked past it six times already; a nondescript gated metal door with no sign on it, cloaked in invisibility. Mental note: it's across from a meat store. The post office is easier to find, mostly because they have a *sign*; that, and it's on the main drag.

We soon get bored of recon, so Jean Lou and I start drinking a beer in every bar that looks lively. I learn that he started walking the Camino in bits and pieces, here and there; he started a few years ago after his marriage fell apart. Around that time, he needed 8 stents in his heart; when he finished rehabilitation, he began to walk the Camino from his home. Not everyone starts in St. Jean Pied de Port, I'm learning. This isn't one of those conversations where I can just chime in with, "Me too! Yeah, I walked here all the way from Canada, including a short swim across the ocean." Frankly, I will be pleased as punch if I can *finish* this damn Camino; I'm no longer interested in extra points or answering the bonus question at the end.

Jean Lou walks like a true Frenchman, but hikes like an SS Gestapo. When he's not hiking, he's walking implacably slow, and stopping every few words to express some vital point. I'm finding it hard to pay attention to what he's saying while also paying attention to where we are going. To be honest, I have no idea where I'm at, whatsoever. I'm totally lost, but that's okay, I have Jean Lou to guide me.

We stop for dinner at a restaurant and meet up with Miriam and Peter from Holland who have been together for 35 years. They hike all over the world together, and this pilgrimage is "just for fun.

Blink.

These are words I haven't had the pleasure of using. I stare at them in awe. Peter is an engineer who works as a consultant for renewable energy. He used to work for a big oil and gas company, but changed jobs because there had to be a better way. I find this impressive. The conversation is very intellectual and I'm enjoying the company as well. Jean Lou works for the Space program in France and is Mr. Somebody Smart. I don't mention I drive a gas guzzling '79 lifted Chevy, nor that I routinely get lost in broad daylight. I'm trying to fit in here. I murmur something to the effect of, "I became a nurse because I wanted to get a degree in something that majored in the highest volume of disgusting bodily secretions as possible. When I'd heard about nursing, I just couldn't tear myself away."

A Japanese hiker and 2 guys from Slovakia arrive. One of the Slovakian men looks so sad it breaks my heart. He tells me he has a great job back home organizing weddings and other large ceremonies, but while everyone is smiling and happy, he himself feels empty. I stay and chat longer because I want to hear more, and I find myself enjoying pilgrim camaraderie. Jean Lou and Japan leave.

Shit. Right. Where am I? Where am I headed again? Oh God, Heather. As if! Wow, and I don't even have a flashlight with me. When I try to head back to my albergue in the dark, I walk as fast as a caterpillar for about 30 minutes before I ask whatever remaining people on the streets where Albergue Zuka is. 12 informers later, I am told the same thing over and over again. There is no albergue by that name that they know of. I explain, "It's the very first one as you walk into town." Nada. I walk down a highway in the dark with cars whizzing by me and realize that I'm heading a direct route back to Pamplona. *Oh, for fuck's sake Heather. Get it together.*

By this point, my "rest" day is shot to hell because I've walked countless miles. Finally, by miracle alone, I get my tipsy ass oriented and start seeing stuff I recognize. And so, by no surprise to me, my albergue is not in fact called 'Zuka' at all. It's Albergue JAKUE. *Tomato, potato.* I reaffirm to myself that "I am a baby sucking off the tits of adventure" when it comes to travel. I used to be good at this once. I run into 6 guys from Wales and spend the rest of the night hanging out with boys half my age. Never in my life have I laughed my ass off so much, so hard, for so long. I must see Wales before I die.

These people are so *real*. We close the bar. I'm not exactly train-wrecked, but I'm close. It's no news flash that I'm the last pilgrim to stumble into my room. I fall asleep in my clothes, face down, and don't bother with a sleeping bag in the pitch black. My feet and legs pulse, so I swallow some Ibuprofen as an afterthought before passing out completely. I have strange dreams during the night, and I wake up melancholic.

CHAPTER 10

Angel of Mercy

DAY 10 October 22 - Dawn

(Puenta La Reina to Estella - 23 km)

I have no time for emotions. I have to get out of this bloody town or I will go crazy.

I stand impatiently outside the shoe store. The man across the cobblestone alley at the *carniceria* tells me that at perhaps 9:30 am the shoe store will open. Shit balls; another late start. I wait and buy some meat and cheese from him because he lets me sit on his bench out of the rain. Oh yes, it is still raining.

The rain in Spain is a pain for my brain. To save time I leave my pack at the meat shop and hurry over to the post office to mail my useless, stinking, filthy, wet boots back to Canada. This puts me back another €40, but I have never been so happy to unload something in my life. Bye, bye, Baby! I hurry back and to my delight the *zapatería* is open for business. Things are looking good in that yes, they do have hiking boots. They just don't have anything larger than a size 7. I throw up my arms and say "But off course you don't!"

I look down at my bare, sandaled feet and start walking the 23 km of slippery mud towards Estella in the pouring rain. I am feeling all kinds of emotions - none of them are happiness. Someone has the gall to wish me a "Buen Camino". I begin to giggle hysterically, which comes out sounding demented. Demented or not, I'm on my way! It's 10:30 am by this point, and I'm not proud of it. I have a beer in every bar I see, *for the struggle*. I meet a gal named Karina from Spain, and she has the most darling, high-pitched, miles-per-hour speech only Spanish women can have. What I mean to say is chipmunks have more baritone and I want to listen to the sound of her voice all the live long day.

I'm surprised at my Spanish; it's appalling, but somehow we are laughing and talking for 30 minutes… of course, almost entirely in English.

About 1 km after lunch I find Tonni stranded at the side of the road, sitting on the ground with his socks off. He's got a bad case of the blisters and has the face of agony to prove it. I give him one of my extra needles and some thread as a gift. I give him a short in-service on how to thread his blisters to help them drain while keeping the wounds open. I also give him some duct tape. I might as well have sun shining out my ass, and he thanks me as if I am the Angel of Mercy — not the blow up doll.

We walk for the rest of the day together, discussing many things. He is from Denmark and is already one of my most favourite walking companions. He offers up his life story to pass the time. We get to Estella fairly late; mostly because I'm slow. He grabs two beds at the albergue while I jet to the shoe store before it closes. Who do I meet there but the Australian man who lost his wallet in Pamplona. We buy the same shoes. "Brothers in arms!" we cheer. Everyone comments on how much weight I'm carrying - like I'm not aware of it. What can I do? I've already mailed back my hairdryer, book and lip gloss, bathing suit… and my boots for that matter. I know I'm ridiculous, but I don't love the attention.

I race back to the albergue in my new galoshes and get substantially lost. It is still shocking to me how I can get so easily turned around. It's a quick recovery thanks to a nice Romanian man with his daughter who take no chances and chaperone me straight to the front door of the hostel. I give the little girl €5 as a tip but she probably deserves more. Tonni has me set up with a bed next to his, but it's a frightening amount of stairs to get up there. I sigh dramatically and tell the refugio owner, "Poco mountania", and he laughs his bloody head off.

The showers are communal but have separate stalls. It's a strange place, this Europe; communal showers are everywhere over here. I'm not totally comfortable with this arrangement, and I stay in my shower stall until Tonni is good and gone before emerging. Jean Lou shows up; I'm assuming by consulting a crystal ball, because I have no idea how he knew I was here. He is staying at a nearby hotel for some much needed pampering, and I tell him he is a very lucky bastard, indeed. He takes Tonni and I out for dinner, where we end up seeing Miriam and Thomas again. I can barely focus on the conversation due to the pain in my whole self, and their high-level conversation is completely lost on me this time. I really just need medical attention for the redness and swelling that is spreading. My wounds are dripping. I want my bed, any bed. It's that simple.

I'm so exhausted I forget to pay, and walk out. Jean Lou calls me back and I am horrified with embarrassment. I cannot believe I just did that! Tonni jokes that because of me all of the future Peregrinos are going to have to pay ahead of their meals; like they do for gasoline in some places.

At the albergue, the dryer isn't working, so all of my clothes are wet and cold. It's humid outside and there is no way these things will dry by morning. This means my pack will be heavier. My feet are terrible, and I feel feverish.

Oh for Christ's sake Heather, quit yer bloody caterwauling.

CHAPTER 11

Soul Shake

DAY 11 October 23

(Estella to Los Arcos - 21km)

I have new shoes. New day! My goal is to *have* a late start. That way I can't be disappointed in myself. Done. I really need a pharmacy, but first, the essentials: a café with pan de chocolate. I take this breakfast with Tonni, and he insists on paying as payment for yesterday's first aid advice. I leave him behind and search for a pharmacy that is supposed to be up about a kilometre away. It is *not* a kilometre away.

Tonni catches up with me at the Fuente del Vino where I'm filling up my water bottle with wine at 9:30 am. I feel 'caught in the act'. The local bodega's donate their leftover wine after bottling to the pilgrims. It is a beautiful gesture, and I'm sure I can speak for everyone here when I say that we deeply relish the sentiment. If no one has ever formally thanked you, bodega people, for this, let me speak on behalf of all past, present, and future pilgrims. We are deeply touched by the generous overture; not to mention it is the coolest thing I have personally ever seen. It's a little early for even me to drink wine, but I am looking forward to having it later on with my lunch. As *if* there is a fountain that pours out wine. If this were in Northern Ontario, nobody would leave the fountain. *Ever.*

It makes for a brilliant photo opportunity. Everyone eventually hikes away from me. I am enjoying the suffering so much that I can't decide which part of me ails the most. All of my parts are calling out to me for attention. There is no sense in complaining, but I do ask God for a pair of wings. I miss my hair dryer. There is a town up ahead, but there's no way of knowing if it's Los Arcos. I try not to give over to excitement. I've had similar mini elations where I've reached a town and then see a sign saying 10 km to go to get to my destination. When that happens, it is soul-smashing.

Today is hot as hell. I'm guessing 25 degrees or more, and my stupid water bottle is filled up with wine. I count my blessings that it's not raining. On the other hand, my puddled DNA has entirely denatured. Hot does not even begin to describe things; the sun is beating down and Los Arcos is a quivering mirage in the distance. I draw in my breath. I probably don't need to beat the dead horse deader by describing what's happening beneath my knees. My body is telling me that this Camino may be pushing my limits. I can't even believe I ran a marathon three months ago, narrowly missing qualification for the Boston Marathon; in the old lady category, that is. *What is wrong with me? It's not as though I'm unfit. This should have been a breeze. Where is the enlightenment? The conversations I'm supposed to have with God? Why don't I have the answers to all of my questions? Where, oh where, is all of my bliss? If this town is the town of blah, blah, blah, and not in fact Los Arcos, I will simply lay my sleeping bag down in the middle of the street.*

It is Los Arcos.

> The king who stole my heart
> sent a message with a butterfly.
> It said, "I am yours"
> and a hundred candles
> burst into flame.
>
> -RUMI

I chose an Austrian albergue that has been run by a lovely couple for the last 3 months. They look at my backpack. I sense initially, they're going to carry it upstairs for me, but thought the better of it not knowing where to begin. I relieve them of the courtesy by plunking it onto my back and climbing up the stairs. I leave them looking dumbfounded. It's because I look like a stick carrying a boulder.

Even when you're done with your hike, you are not really done with your day. I need a shower, but instead, I choose to drop my bag and cruise the town. It's the first time I've arrived somewhere while it's still daylight, and I want to explore. I also want a beer the size of Texas and to take my shoes off. I brush off the other pilgrims for now because I want an hour or so alone to write in my journal and chill out. It's okay to be antisocial right? I hide in the corner of a bar and eat a feast of calamari. I write copious amounts, while sipping a cold one. Eventually, I am found. "Mass is at 7:00 pm, Heather." "Oh, for sure," I smile to my pilgrim informer. A few minutes alone and I feel centered again. Restored. I am essentially an introvert trapped in an extrovert's body.

But first, I need to get to a pharmacia.

I buy €36 worth of foot care products, and I feel fairly confident about my loot. Some pilgrims tease me because they are trying to meet a daily budget of €10. I can't even imagine how that could be done seeing as I have a ten-euro-a-day foot care regimen. I get back in time for some Spanish sangria and then we all rush off to mass.

I brace myself for the worst. I have never felt spectacularly comfortable in a Catholic church. This is because I have sure-as-shootin' been burned at the stake in a previous lifetime.

As I enter the church, I am stunned quiet in a number of ways. The first being that it is the most beautiful structure I have ever entered. The detail and gold overwhelm me, the statues, arches, and ceilings are painted in a way that reminds me of Michelangelo. This is the most worthwhile place I've seen to photograph, but alas, I have left my camera at the albergue. I feel completely present and doubt I will need a photo to remember this night anyway.

The second thing I'm immediately aware of is the energy of the place. I could feel how many others had been in this very spot before me. There is a regal heaviness to it mixed with so much love. You can almost taste the specialness. I feel acutely aware of my being a foreigner in my sandals and filthy clothes, but somehow it's not only accepted, but respected. During the Spanish service, I hear the words *peregrino, Santiago, The Way, Compostela*, and I am overtaken by emotion. The service is for us! We, the pilgrims, are asked to stand and to come forward.

The priest asks us where we are from and he recites *The Pilgrims Prayer* with us.

Prayer of the Pilgrims

Lord, you who recalled your servant Abraham out of the town UR in Chaldea and who watched over him during all his wanderings; you who guided the Jewish people through the desert; we also query to watch your present servants, who for love for your name, make a pilgrimage to Santiago de Compostela.

Be for us,
A companion on our journey,
The guide on our intersections,
The strengthening during fatigue,
The fortress in danger,
The resource on our itinerary,
The shadow in our heat,
The light in our darkness,
The consolation during dejection,
And the power of our intention,

So that we under your guidance, safely and unhurt, may reach the end of our journey, and strengthened with gratitude and power, secure and filled with happiness, may join our home.
For Jesus Christ, Our Lord. Amen.

Apostle James, pray for us.
Holy Virgin, pray for us.

I can't stop the flow of tears. I feel God's embrace in my heart. I am given understanding that He acknowledges what I'm doing, but that I don't have to do it. I'm experiencing God. I'm talking with him in my very soul. I can hear him loud and clear and it bowls me over with humility. I'm touched by the message to me. I am so humbled by it that it reinforces why I need to do it. I DO have to walk this. I want God to know how grateful I am; I want to prove it with my suffering *now*, not just for the suffering in my past. I need to do it for myself, as well. I need to know that I am well.

I'm wondering if my spiritual journey is also a religious one. But that confuses me. I tried religion and it didn't suit me. I walk out of the church in a daze and I can't quite pull it together. I want a calming cigarette, but when I ask if it's okay to light up I feel judged by another pilgrim. I want to cry some more. I beg off that I'm feeling a little bit cold, and steal away into the night.

At the albergue, I sit outside in a darkened patio and give myself permission to cry, sob, and exorcise demons, or whatever. I'm not sure what's upsetting me, only that something needs to get out. I know some of it is the weighty responsibility of the pilgrim is becoming real. It's not "just a walk"; it's not just a vacation. Physically, I'm a hot mess, and yet each day I persevere. Am I on autopilot, deciding to continue forward, regardless of the cost? After the service tonight, I don't even know for sure if I'm the one making decisions here. Something is pushing me from behind, within, and then pulling me onward. I am emotionally exhausted. I'm barely able to engage in the minimum required conversation with my roommates before I drop off into the worst sleep of my life.

CHAPTER 12

Dream Bigger

DAY 12 Oct. 24

(Los Arcos to Viana)

I am a new woman. This is my best walking day thus far and it flies by in a jiffy.

I walk with Sheri, of no fixed address, USA. She is thinking of moving to France to be with her lover. Her story is amazing and her life is in a catapult of transition. We spend the day discussing spirituality. She has this ability to verbalize things in a way I have never been able to. I want to write everything she says down on paper. Better yet, I wish our conversations could be recorded, so I could hear her wisdom again and again. She has learned much, and has had many gurus in this life.

She explains to me that everything we need is already within ourselves. If this is true, then I should be able to manifest new heel skin for my feet - on the double. She tells me to "watch and see what turns up from the world. It will be better than anything your mind could dream up. If you know yourself, the most perfect things, people, experiences reveal themselves". It sounds like magic. I think I should wish for more than heel skin from the universe. Note to self: I need to get dreaming bigger… *way* bigger.

What is it that I really want from the Universe?

Why don't I know?

Sheri continues to tell me to write down what I know for sure, but also to realize that all beliefs and things we know can change and evolve. It's good to set some boundaries while following intuition. *Boundaries? I'm terrible with boundaries!* Our conversation can't be summed up into 2 or 3 lines, but I did come away from it feeling as though I might already be doing some of these things. That's refreshing, because for the past week or so I have been feeling like a physical, mental, and spiritual fledgling.

Regardless, I should really get a guru.

Where does one get one of those?

We talk about our relationships and how they affect us. I don't have a relationship, so my story is shorter than hers by about 30 minutes. I tell her about Grizzly and the complexities withstanding – mostly around him not wanting me. I tell her about the dream I had in Puenta La Reina. The dream I couldn't bear to write down immediately, or acknowledge.

In the dream, Grizzly came to me, and our souls were able to communicate in ways that we were never able to in real life. I felt how much he loved me; we played and flew through the air together, holding hands. My heart was filled with so much love that I thought I would burst. This is how I knew it could be for us. Then, in the very next moment, I felt him fade away from me. His eyes lost their focus, his energy became overtaken by a room filled with loud people and chaos. I called out to him, but he didn't seem to recognize me. He looked so sad and so very lost. He was energy-less and I knew then that he was lost to me forever. When I awoke, I was gasping for air and weeping.

The parallel to the reality of this situation is astonishing and it leaves me entirely discombobulated. The dream just won't fade from my head or my heart. I don't know how to process this information. Is it merely symbolic, or is he in trouble?

When we get to our destination, Sheri and I check into the local albergue. I feel physically fantastic, but mentally wiped out. I fall asleep on the 3rd bunk (as if they have that) and subsequently drool all over myself. Once rested, I am ravenous, and I realize I haven't eaten much in the last day or so. I head to the bar and choke down a surprisingly tasteless bocadillo sandwich.

I'm hit with the glaring fact that if I keep going at a snail's pace, I will be 3 days short of Santiago when my train for France pulls away. I'm experiencing pilgrim stress. I'm going to have to walk 25-30 km per day to reach my goal, if I want to achieve the Compostela. I have to start considering what this trek will mean if my pilgrimage finishes at a different end point. Amidst all of my shenanigans, I've lost too many days. I don't want to call them 'lost days', but even if I have no more setbacks, it's possible I won't receive a formally signed Compostela. I think I may not have the stamina to do 25-30 km days, but I have not given up all hope just yet. I had entertained the possibility that I might not make it to Finisterre, but never had it occurred to me that I might not make it to Santiago. *Why is this so important to me? Is this a box I need checked off as completed? Even God said I didn't need to do it. Honestly Heather, if that's not a hall pass, I don't know what is.*

The Camino is far more punishing than I had imagined, plain and simple. I thought it was a no brainer, actually. I'm fit, I'm mentally strong. I have to start being okay with alternate endings in general, not just with my little hiking dilemmas.

Sheri and I head into the village to procure food stuffs for the morning and to check out dinner options. We hear church bells and decide to go to mass together. This pilgrim service is even more of a spiritual assault than the previous soul shaking service. I'm tearful from the get-go, and there are no dry spells at all for the duration. I'm a bit of a spectacle, but I am powerless to pull it together.

The priest shakes my hand, and I begin to sob uncontrollably. I'm trembling and releasing something monumental. What, specifically, I cannot say. I don't even feel sad or lost. It's more of a sweeping emotion, and in this moment I'm hit with another realization of some higher power acknowledging me. I do realize that I sound like a crazy person right now.

I shall, however, take it to my grave that He was thanking *me* for thanking *Him* of all things, and blessing my journey.

To be acknowledged for struggles I've traversed over the last ten years, and perhaps all of my life, is humbling to say the least. An energy surges through my every molecule like a rocket, shaking me physically. Is this the Kundalini experience that I had read about? The one I had experienced years prior in Sedona, Arizona? At that time, a gypsy woman had passed a large white crystal over me, leaving my body to shake like an earthquake was passing through. She said something to the effect that I would need this, "for later on"; something about unleashing my Kundalini. I didn't understand what she meant at the time. I was frightened and I begged her to stop. Fourteen years later, it's happening again. This time, I am not frightened. I am curious and humbled. It is something I am ready to investigate further.

What is happening to me? There aren't any words in the English language to describe what has happened here, and my scientific brain is at a loss. All I know for sure is I am loved beyond belief. There is something out there that is really, really good. Someone who knows our intentions and our hearts and better still, is cheering us on! This experience is *forcing* me to feel love so that I know what love really feels like.

Trusting love has been difficult for me. When the real thing hits you in the face, it really does help you to remember for future reference. The feeling is all-embracing and unmistakeable. It's forgiving, reliable, and fatherly. I stay in my pew and sob it all out while I let the past go. I feel lighter than I have in years.

Disoriented when I come back to my senses, I wonder *what in the Sam Hill just happened back there? That was marvellous!*

Thankfully, Sheri stays with me. She is quiet too. We can't even speak to one another but I'm guessing she gets what has just gone down. We find a restaurant, and though wanting to be alone together in this, we end up joining a Peregrino table. It was probably the best thing for us, in retrospect. I'm still a teensy bit misty eyed but no one judges me this time. Everyone has had their moments by now, I expect. There is a collective understanding; we have all been emotionally excavated.

CHAPTER 13

Tender, Loving, Care

DAY 13 October 25
(Viana to Villarosa 30+/-km)

It's going to be another 10 hour day, but I'm motivated to keep chipping away at the old grindstone. My feet are ruined and my left leg is still swollen, but it may have improved the slightest bit: the redness seems to be receding. Two girls from, "way-the-fuck-north of Dryden, Ontario" ask me to eat breakfast with them. We have beautiful local eggs, and cheese with bread. I call them Trail Angels and they are the epitome of adorable. It's the best meal of the day and it keeps me going for the rainy miles ahead.

I get in step with Kevin from Australia. He is an older gentleman with the most wonderful giggle. He spends 4 months a year travelling, now that he is retired. His feet look frightening, but I am no expert. The first few miles are agony, but then everything sort of blissfully numbs as we go along. This is what we tell ourselves, anyhow.

Kevin asks me to pull 2 cards: one from each of his decks of meditation cards. The first card I pull says *Tenderness*, and the next card says *Love*. I tell him I believe I have pulled the wrong cards, and he chuckles long and hard. He tells me, "Oh no, Heather, they aren't wrong at all. You are a Nurse. You already know how to care, but Heather, are you tender and loving towards yourself?" I feel more than a little irritated at first (which makes him chuckle more) before I realize he is 110% right on the money. I can't even imagine spending a day meditating how to be tender and loving to myself. The whole thing seems absurd. At the same time, on a more visceral level, it's likely true. I thank him for his insight, but inside I am absolutely stewing with anger though I'm not sure why.

I have to leave Kevin behind due to his feet and his probably knowing how to be tender and loving towards himself. He is going to call it a day. I give him a *caring* hug for his wisdom, and we part on the best of terms. Later in the day, I happen to look up and see a lamppost with the letters T.L.C. painted on it. I nearly trip onto my face. T.L.C as in....Tender, Loving Care? This confirms for me Kevin's earlier prediction that I need to meditate on these words. Despite the lamppost reminder, it won't be an easy task for me.

Everyday while I walk, people wish me a buen Camino. Every stranger smiles at me, or at least says, "Hola, buenas dias." It is a very polite country.

I begin to walk with Janice (from Minnesota), who lost her husband a year ago at the age of 62. She tells me she is grieving and trying to get over her guilt for not being nicer to him while he was alive. She didn't realize until he was gone what a wonderful husband he really was. I listen to her and allow her to cry for as long as she needs. We spend hours lost in conversation, putting one foot in front of the other. We surprise ourselves when we realize that we have walked 20 km together. I think about what she has said about appreciating the people you love. I need to do a better job telling them; showing them. I continue on to the next town, Ventosa, and she stays in Navarrete. I don't see Janice again on the Camino.

I stop in a bar and order a beer. There is an African Grey parrot in a cage, off in the corner. He's chatty and beautiful and reminds me of Link. Link was an African Grey that I had for years until I passed him on to a friend who needed some company. I had to give him away because I wasn't doing a spectacular job of taking care of him *or* myself. I really wanted him to have a better life but it felt like amputation to let him go. I send him a mental kiss.

There are many canary cages in the towns I pass, and the sounds please me. Today must be bird day because as I passed a lake earlier with Janice, the ducks were making quacking noises that sounded like laughter. It had made us both laugh just listening to them.

I see two Husky dogs that remind me of my own Husky, Annoushka, a.k.a. Noosh. I sure as heck miss my dog who is a brown and blue eyed beauty. She would love a long stroll like this. All the dogs here are smaller mixed breeds, so seeing Huskies around seems about as expected as finding a giraffe wandering around New York City.

It's a hard push on to Villarosa. The last 5 km of every day is punishing, and my feet are splintering. Each little stone in this pebbly-ass road seems to bruise the bones in my feet. I'm compensating in a comically, unnatural gait; it is quite unbecoming.

Truth is, I'm a listing ship.

There really isn't anywhere civilized to pee along the Camino. It's always a risk when you pull your pants down. It's inevitable some farmer or Peregrino will march along right in the middle of your morning glory and say, "Hola!" My luck must be improving because I water the earth this time without interruption. Lotteries come many different packages.

When I get to Villarosa, I think I've walked 30 +/- km; not that I have an inkling without a map. I'm positive that I cannot go another step, when the albergue appears out of nowhere. *Thank you, thank you, thank you!* It is very nice and clean, though I would have certainly settled for less. The hospitalero is from Austria, and she insists on helping me to my room. There is a washer and a working dryer, and I am overjoyed to say the least. I have nothing that isn't a reeking, putrid mess. I pull a 'France' and go to dinner with only my jacket and long johns on.

I meet two Israeli people who invite me to a home cooked meal. I accept wholeheartedly, since there is no bar or restaurant in this town. Since I don't want to eat my coat or long johns, I have two heaping platefuls of vegetarian food. Trail Angels are turning up everywhere. I accept their contact information in case I end up in Israel someday. Really, you just never know.

They speak perfect English and I feel extremely comfortable with them. They have seven children back home and just love feeding pilgrims. That's great because I need all the love and tenderness I can get!

After supper, as I'm continuing with the laundry situation, I hear this tragically awful music. A large group of German folk is doing a Christian Camino, and they are singing mercilessly to an out-of-tune Ukulele. They *have* to know they are terrible! The cacophony of horrendousness is ear-blistering, and they are using sheet music for this. I'd bet my bottom dollar that right this very minute, angels are trying to cover their ears by cutting off their wings. I should be more sensitive having had my own spiritual experience, but their activity feels pushy and the rest of us are just trying to unwind from the day's lessons. This nightmare trumps a previous albergue by a hundred thousand miles, wherein the hospitalero blasted Gregorian chant music at 6:30 in morning to wake up the pilgrims.

That *is not* T.L.C.

That is torture!

It's becoming bizarro world over here, and I can't wait to get the *bleep, bleep, bleep* out of here.

I pack up at the speed of light and eat breakfast with the Israelis before I hit the road running (well, who am I kidding here - there was no running). I have close to 35 km to accomplish today. I've gone *loco cabeza* overnight if I think I can do this; the ukulele has tipped me over the edge.

CHAPTER 14

The Pilgrim's Stone

DAY 14 October 26

(Villarosa to Santo Domingo)

Is it any surprise that it's raining and as dark as soot outside? Granted, it is only 7:40 am. I pull out my brand new, never-been-used Petzl headlamp, which turns out to be the worst thing I've ever spent money on. There is a *plewf* of pale light, but I can't actually see my shoes.

Within 45 minutes, I've managed to get lost three times. I'm getting the picture: I'm not supposed to be hiking in the dark. Thank goodness for locals who pity the pilgrims, otherwise I would be in Penticton by now. They spin us right around in the correct direction and get us back on The Way. They say the Camino always provides. I spend the rest of the day getting lost, and then found.

Most towns have in the neighbourhood of a bazillion trail markers. That fact has been fairly reliable until now, where the going is substantially sketchier. I take my first rest stop in Navarette. It is a very poor town, but I find a bar that has great music playing. This is fantastic because music is not free on the radio airwaves like it is in other countries. Most places in Spain won't muster up the pluck to provide it for patrons. I feel a little racy because of it, and treat myself to a café con leche and a pan con chocolate. I savour this ambrosia in a stupor of musical flavour Heaven. Food = Sanity, and I forget where I am for a time. I write a bit in my journal, and when I'm good and rested, I put my boots back on and hump onward. It's true: I have started removing footwear in restaurants now. This is a new abysmal low. It's called *I don't give a hoot. I'm a Pilgrim, and I need this.* People seem to either shut a blind eye or appear sympathetic.

I hit the pharmacy and a market where I stock up on supplies. If wine were freeze dried, I'd have gotten some of that as well. In Najera, I walk a short time with Nicol, from France. He thinks I'm 25. This is my best compliment so far and I will take it, thank you very much! My pace today is power-slow and he's out of sight in no time. I miss having the company but the rest of the day I hike alone.

It's pouring rain and I'm freezing. I've long since switched out my shoes for my sandals, and my hands are a lovely shade of blue. I just want to get to Santo Domingo. I'm sick of singing made up jingles in my head, and I've had to evacuate my bowels for the last 6 hours or so. There is *literally. Nowhere*!

Should I go on? I'm hypothermic and wishing the road to Santiago was made of rose petals and memory foam. I think tonight I will remove my legs like Barbie and set them on the night table till morning. Give them a good little rest. I walk through miles of industrial zone in Santo Domingo. I ask you, *anyone*: IS THERE AN ALBERGUE IN THIS TOWN? I look homeless.

I *am* homeless.

But get this: I am *not* lost!

I picked up a rock today. There are cairns of rock piles all along the Camino. People say you need to pick up a stone or two along the Way to Santiago. When you feel it is the right time, you simply leave the rock behind imbedded with all of your troubles and sins, freeing you to move forward in your life. It's to let go of the past, thus healing old wounds. I thought I could do this in my head instead of having to actually pick up a stone at all. This is the conversation I have with myself.

My, how evolved you are, Heather.

You are not, however, in the ADVANCED SPIRITUALITY class.

No?

You don't have the requirements completed.

This is a REMEDIAL class -101 and you, Heather, are on the short bus.

You need a GURU, a guide, and the blessings of a thousand saints.

The least you could do is pick up a stone.
How about the stone that was given to you back in Canada; that reared its head time and time again? Beckoning you, mocking you, challenging you to do all of this in the first place? What did you do with that rock?

I dunno?

I guess I forgot it at home.

Jesus, Heather! How could you forget it?

Scolding myself doesn't make me feel better so I change direction.

Really? What's the main problem here?

There are stones all over the place.

Just PICK ONE!

I've been seeing signs of 4 all day, so I needed a square rock. Today's landscape reminds me of New Mexico, where I lived for 10 years. More specifically, I lived right at the Four Corners. I think of the 4 directions (in which I blindly go each day), the 4 seasons, the 4 chambers of the heart (tenderness & love), my favourite number is 44, and one of my passwords is 4444. Need I go on? My found stone is a square one with four distinct sharp corners. So there it is. I've picked up a rock today.

I get to the albergue at 6:30 pm. I've been on the road to Santiago for 11 hours today. I feel as though I've carried the Holy Cross on my back. I am *not* a Sherpa; nor am I a mule. This being a pilgrim is not for the faint of heart. Why did I think this would be easy? Was it my idea to do this? Who can I blame? Myself?

The problem with showing up to town late in the day is there's no time to explore. The Camino has been all-encompassing. I guess what I am *not* is a sightseer. Some of the pilgrims made it in 4 hours earlier. I know it's not a contest but it is disagreeable to me that I am the last pilgrim every single day. It has been suggested that perhaps I'd like to have my luggage transported ahead to the next town. There are so many that do this they say, however, I have yet to see anyone without a backpack.

Rumour has it that some people do the Camino by car, leave the engine running, get their required pilgrim passport stamp in each town, and then speed away to luxurious hotels. I've taken to calling these phantom pilgrims Cappuccino Pilgrims. They sound like really smart pilgrims to me.

I don't want the Compostela at all if I don't finish. All I know for sure is that I will eventually get to Santiago because my train leaves from there. By the time I arrive at the albergue, I'm tiptoeing.

I'm ready for the slaughter house.

A long walk down a plank.

Take me down to the river.

Toss me onto the wood pile.

Oh for Christ's sake, just shoot me dead.

THE PILGRIM'S STONE

My nubs-called-feet are tenderized by stones from the road, but I reckon with the right spices and cooked at 350 degrees could be delicious for someone. Except for the fact they smell like sewer gas.

The water in the shower is a sensational *hot-as-Hell* that I deeply relish. I wash my socks and underwear in there, even though it says on a very large sign that doing so is "forbidden". I *donativo* €10, which I'm hoping brings me heavenly absolution. I've forgotten my dry socks in my room so I put my wet socks back on and head over to dinner.

Dinner is probably only 25 meters away, but I consider phoning a taxi. I head past the bar and into the restaurant at the back. I'm alone, like most of today, but I'm pleased with the solitude. Wait!

These socks must come OFF!!

I lay them down on the chair beside me and remove my shoes. I'm barefoot on the cold tile, but it is cleaner than anything I've stepped on today. I see the waitress' eyes widen in disbelief staring at my hamburgery feet.

I'm culpable.

She serves me this ridiculous amount of food and enough wine to float me home to Canada, then tops it all off with a bill so small I can palpate her pity. I decide it's best if I don't overstay my welcome and hurry myself along, since the restaurant is filling up with locals. Suddenly, I don't blend. I pay with as much dignity as possible, and I walk out holding my socks.

Ohhh, my sweet Jesus!!

Is that those PEOPLE?

Please tell me I'm not...

Do I hear ukulele?!.

CHAPTER 15

Dreams

DAY 15 October 27

(Goal: Santo Domingo to Villa Franca)

So that didn't happen. I did not make it to Villa Franca. In the frosty albergue, I trade my skinny granola bar with Lil Sam (from Boston) for his boiled egg, and I continue eating whatever scraps I discover in my bag. Things are grim. I think he knew I didn't have anything to rave about and gifted me his egg. What I'm trying to get at is, an egg tends to keep a person full for a time; but a granola bar burns itself off before you've even tied up your shoelaces. The egg feels like charity. I pretend on the surface that it is a fair trade, even though I know it's not. He gave me an edge. Sam, at 18 years of age, seems more evolved than I am. That right there is unfair.

6.5 km into the day I am ready for a stop in Granon. When I get there, I start my day over right and slam 2 coffees back to back with my usual chocolate croissant to fortify. One of the perks of walking everyday is being able to eat and drink as much as you want of whatever you want, while your body sculpts itself into the best shape it has ever been. I'm still thinking about the egg, but Sam is long gone. I'm not about to donate my kidneys or anything, but I felt I should say thank you again.

Need I mention that it is windy outside with a large helping of pouring rain; it's freezing and I'm in a blistery Hell. One of my more brilliant ideas to travel in late fall. On second thought, I admit that I'd rather the weather be a little on the cold side than hot; which I think could be worse. I may be Canadian but I still want to be in bed with a heating blanket out of this bastardly weather. That's my bed back in Canada, if anyone can hear me, and has a magic wand handy.

I talk with Misha who is Swiss, but looks Asian. He's done the Camino and is back in Granon to work in the albergue, to fund his lifestyle. His lifelong dream is to walk around the world and I query inwardly how he will pay for that kind of adventure. I am aware of his serenity. There is a nice energy to him. I have to move on but I could have easily stayed and talked the day away about our spiritual paths. He gives me his card and tells me he has a GoFundMe page for his walk around the world. He wants other people to pay for him? I can think of about 50 people off-hand that need a GoFundMe page more than this guy. People enduring real life tragedies who would never dream of asking others to pay their way. As I walk out of the bar there is a trash barrel at the door. I covertly toss his card in the receptacle as I leave. It's all so disappointing.

By the time I make it to the next town, I'm soaked and shivering. It's only 3:30 pm but I order the Pilgrim Dinner and I eat everything that Senora puts in front of me. I need to keep going since I have only walked 23 km today and Santiago is still a long way off. I end my day around 28 km, with my hamstrings about to snap in two. I really can't go on. Fatigue is mounting on different levels. The Camino is not only catching up with me, but it has caught me fair and square, and thrown me over its back.

I meet up with other pilgrims I've met before, and we chat and eat like starved prisoners. Another Pilgrim Dinner, *por favor*; my legs must be hollow. The albergue I want to stay at is an old hospital from 1514 and its sole purpose these days is for pilgrims. It's *donativo* or rather *pay-by-donation*, and there are no beds. I'm taken by surprise when they welcome me in. When I heard there were no beds, I had assumed they were full. Not so. They really just don't have any beds in the building at all, for whatever reason. To my delight I am given a yoga mat to sleep on in the attic, where I will later sleep in my thermals with my hat and mitts on. It's bliss up here even though I can see my breath. To be honest, I'm just grateful to be indoors for the night.

I'm handed a pamphlet regarding a monastery in Burgos where women can stay. I'm tempted to go and check it out. For some reason, the idea is intriguing to me but I'm nervous about it. Surrounded by nuns might illuminate how far off the beaten track my soul is. I'm not sure I can face that right now. *Why all of this fear? Is my soul so blackened that I cannot be forgiven? No. That's not it. Could it be that it would force me to live more authentically, more spiritually, more, more, more? Live?*

I want to mention a dream I had a few nights ago: I dreamt about my friend Margaret back home. She is standing at the top of some stairs and wearing a black robe with her hair cut short. She's surrounded by light. She is smiling and in every way, looks reborn. She is absolutely stunning, which she already is in real time, but there is a glow about her that speaks to me of happiness and peace. I share this dream to another pilgrim to see if she might solve its meaning for me. She explains that it could be about Margaret and some transformation that's surrounding her, but it's more likely regarding me. If that's true, then why didn't I just put myself in the dream? Why is everything cloak and dagger around here?

I've had many dreams while on The Way, and most of them have been disturbing. I've remembered an old recurring dream that spanned from 6 years old into my twenties: I'm being chased down a country road near my grandmother's house, and when I turn around to see who is behind me, I see the flash of a butcher's knife and the face of my mother. For years, I would wake from this dream terrified. It's probably obvious this is one of the strained relationships in my life. What I want to know is the significance of recurring dreams. The dream stopped around the time I moved out of my parent's home. Was I a burden? Or did I remind my mother of the life she didn't reach out and go for?

My siblings admitted mother to the psychiatric ward for carrying around a butcher's knife when my father had mentioned he felt uneasy being around her. How long had this been going on? When my siblings caught her doing this, we had to wonder if she was planning to harm my father. She had already done so many questionable things by that point. What stressors drove her to do that? Was my father to blame somehow? Or was my mother hitting her rock bottom by way of mental illness?

There is a lot of confusion surrounding this and other things, but what I can say with confidence is this; I think everyone in my family did the best that they could with what tools they had at the time. You can't always Humpty Dumpty things back together, so I'm gift wrapping the family into a box and putting it in my mental basement for now. There is only so much I'm willing to work on at the moment.

The other women in the attic choose to sleep downstairs in the lounge where there is more heat. They encourage me to join them but I chose to stay in the frozen attic. I'm not sure exactly why I often choose solitude over companionship. I've always been able to refuel better alone; too much time with other people's energy seems to drain my own. Alone on the floor, in the freezing attic, I realize that I am grateful that I listened to my own rhythm. It ends up being the best sleep I've had on the Camino. Sometimes intuition is so *intuitive*.

CHAPTER 16

Don't Judge a Book by its Cover

DAY 16 October 28

(Villa Franca to Tosantos)

Breakfast is lively and filled with such a marvellous energy. It's as if these pilgrims and I have been friends for many a long year. I know only half of their names, but it doesn't seem to matter in the slightest. I head out on the Way. Today is special because it is not only raining, but there is a splendid mix of sleet and snow. I stop and make a bonhomme de neige with my Spanish friend, Aurie. We communicate in English with a splash of Spanish.

I must learn Spanish. I keep travelling to Spanish countries, and my Spanish is worse than a three year old. Aurie is not my kind of gorgeous, but his eyes are, and I could literally drink them up. I think it is the mystic quality about him that is so compelling. What is it about the eyes that reveals and disguises. I think of Grizzly's eyes and I wonder what is hiding behind them. What does he think? Why doesn't he say? He has his secrets and I'm certain I wouldn't want to know what they are. I have this habit of choosing guys with secrets. This has to stop. It's downright madness.

I lag behind but another group of friends catch up with me. It is Sam and some sweet Korean girls with Coske from Japan. They pull me along with their positivity. The conversation is as easy as it is hilarious. Their youth buoys me. I do my best to keep up with them, but after an hour or so I fall behind again. I don't much mind being left behind because I never leave myself behind. I'm doing this walk for me and the big guy upstairs. I walk my own pace. Eventually, at this pace, I should arrive at... someplace.

I stop for lunch and fill my gullet up to the max. I keep on with my meandering another 3 km, so that tomorrow is that much easier for me. Use energy when you have the energy, I say. A few other pilgrims are moving towards Atapuerca. They want to see a museum of paleontology and archaeology. It being Sunday and tomorrow being a holiday, I'm not sure there will be much for them to see. I wish them well with their endeavour because unless there is a rail car, I'm not going.

It's every possible inclement weather outside and frankly, I'm tired of it. I drop my bag unceremoniously onto the floor and head to the bar with friends. It is a regular occurrence that people you have met on the trail often meet up again and again at various points. We all have different steps and different setbacks which allow our paths to crisscross. It makes for interesting palaver in the evenings; as difficulties are regaled over glasses of ruby red wine. The significance of this is that I must be catching up in some way, as others are slowing down. I know it's not a contest but no one likes to be last and that includes hiking all the way up to spiritual growth. Maybe this old turtle will yet become the hare.

I have a nagging regret about yesterday, and I vow never to make this mistake again in my life: the albergue that had no beds had a donativo box at the door. I guess because there were no beds or heat, I "cheaped" out for the first time on the Camino and put in a smaller amount than I normally do. These hosts were charitable and kind to me! They expected little and gave us pilgrims so much in return. I'm plagued with guilt, because I've just realized that my money will affect the next pilgrims that come along. The hosts held a prayer service last night that clarified a lot of questions I had had about being a pilgrim. I was given 2 meals, wine, hot showers, and a lovely peaceful energy that permeated the grounds. I didn't realize this when I entered and I was hasty to judge it as a dive. It ended up being rejuvenating and a wonderful experience for me. I must do better going forward and not judge a book by its cover.

CHAPTER 17

Let Go Of Thinking

DAY 17 October 29

(Tosantos to Atapuerca 30.2 km)

Surprise. Rain. Cold. Wind. All things considered, I feel great. I think that last night's albergue experience and sleep were the best I've ever had. I walk part of the day with Aurie (who I've nicknamed the Mushroom Man). He is shy, but speaks better English than he lets on. I enjoy the walk and his company. He has a peaceful composure to him which soothes me. I do well to be around peaceful people as opposed to the swirly, whirly people. I have a tendency to absorb the energy of people whose energy doesn't suit my own. It lambastes me. I get somehow wrapped up in their life drama and it can take days for me to shake it off. My energy seems to drain out of me as though I've been bitten by an emotional vampire. Note to self: hang around calm, sedated, or dead people.

It starts to sleet enough snow to make a snowball and Aurie makes a tiny bonhomme de neige for me. We lose one another after a few hours because of a stop I make to change my socks, and *comer* (eat). He fades from view and I wonder if he was actually real at all.

> Put your thoughts to sleep,
> Do not let them cast a shadow
> over the moon of your heart.
> Let go of thinking.
>
> –RUMI

There is a forest on both sides of the road and it looks like row upon row of perfect Christmas trees. I drink in the beauty for as long as I dare and then urge myself onward. Despite this beauty, I resent myself for being a whiner all the time. My internal dialogue is incessant and I am annoying myself. I haven't been complaining out loud, but I sure am unleashing my darkness into my mind and these pages. Maybe that is the best way, but I still want to get out of my head somehow. It must be far better to reconcile suffering on the inside than bleed the ears of others; however, I yearn for mental toughness just the same. Why can't I just let go of all the thinking? I want to be one of those people who can transcend silly things like pain... like Rumi... and Jesus.

I'm still pondering if I can keep going when the Camino sends me a gift: a gaggle of my trail children, as I call them, turn up and sheppard me along with their happiness. The point is not lost on me. They entertain me for hours and as they start to drift away, I smile to myself because I can still hear their giggles. I know I can do it now thanks to them, and I am grateful for their little pull-along. As I'm rolling into Ayer, I stop for a hamburger and beer even though I need to walk another 2 or 3 km, before I can end my day. In the meantime, I have plenty of time to chill with the trail children that I have caught up with.

The wind is biting cold and the last thing I want to do is to go back out there. I end up enjoying the solo hike after all, so it was time well spent. There is a moment of confusion for me because I see figures coming towards me that I recognize. They have no packs on. It doesn't make any sense. Am I going the wrong way again? They are off to see the Atapuerca museum that I had heard about. I join them; why not? What's an extra 2 km give or take. It turns out that most of the museum is closed. There is some irony in arriving at one of the world's most celebrated sites, with not a thing available for us to see. I remind myself that I'm not a tourist. I'm here to bust up bad Karma.

Missing out on the museum doesn't upset me. I'm here for a Camino and I'm realizing that's all I can manage to do right now. I might as well focus and do it right. I want to meet myself square on, and there is no photograph for that. Come to think of it, I haven't taken a photo in days. It doesn't seem all that important anymore. Sometimes hours go by where I don't even raise my head to look at what's around me. I get engrossed in my thoughts, the sound of my steps, and what my soul is trying to tell me. It takes all of my energy *to pay attention*.

At the town of Atapuerca, I am delighted. I've somehow managed to catch up with Tonni; the Slovak fellas, Roman and Pauli; the Aussie bloke, James; and li'l Aurie. We go for a drink at the bar and break some bread together with Danielle (Toronto), and Mike (USA). The moon is full and the world appears to be laying itself at our feet. Tonni is dumbfounded that I caught up to everyone. I admit that I'm as surprised as he is that I'm still in the game. Without thinking, completely reflexly, I hear myself say, "Things are going a tiny bit smoother for me". *Why did I say that? Could it be true?*

I'm tuckered right out and I'm three days behind in my journal; I need to get down to business. The Hospitalero hasn't shown up to the albergue yet, so I just grab an empty bed and hit the sack with a *kerplunk*. I need a stamp and to pay, but the man is nowhere to be found. Blurred by fatigue, I'm able to shake off responsibility. Luckily, tomorrow is another day.

Mind

(Burgos to Leon - The Meseta)

> I asked, "What should I do?"
> He said, that is the question.
> I said, "Is that all you can say?"
> He said, Seeker, always keep asking,
> "What should I do?"
>
> –RUMI

SECTION 2 -

MIND: The MIND section of the pilgrimage speaks to the mental struggle hikers experience midway through their journey. It becomes a test of mental fortitude, sanity, and composure. Many pilgrims call it *Meseta Madness*.

CHAPTER 18

Self-Sacrifice and EGO

DAY 18 October 30

(Atapuerca to Burgos 20 km /-)

7:00 am Shit... get up! No hospitalero. No stamp. No pay. Shit.
    I go to the bar and get a bar stamp, which will have to do. I leave some money on the counter at the albergue and hope it falls into the right hands. I have breakfast with the girls, briefly meet someone named Marco from England, and I am out the door.

I walk alone for hours on craggy rock and rolling hills. It's a stunning beauty that refreshes my mind. I wonder if this is what Scotland looks like. There is a large cross at the top of a hill, stark and alone, and I wish I knew why. It is times like this that I wish I had a guidebook handy. I'm humming a tune of I-don't-know-what, and I feel happiness all through me.

I stop for a hot coffee in a town that I didn't see a sign for, and sit with Kath, Marcos, and Veronica. We hike the rest of the day together. I'm slow and they are in agony with their backs, so we stop at a park in Burgos and I massage them with deep heat and do some physiotherapy for them. I've been carrying Marcos' pack on the front of me for the past 10 km. He wants to quit and Veronica is in tears. I feel so bad for them. Every pilgrim has their share of bad days. I offer to carry more of their gear, as it's the first day I'm not walking on the balls of my feet. Wait. What am I doing? Am I crazy? Is this compassion, or is this my ego? I am a sucker for the sick and the lame because I am the sick and the lame. Is that the point? To truly understand suffering and compassion, we must suffer, ourselves?

This is could also be more of my self-sacrificing behaviour. I'm famous for this kind of charity and in the end it has always been to my detriment. I can't help it. I allow myself to get reeled in and then ooze out my life force in a steady stream to people. Some of the time it is worthy people that I help, but in recent years I seem to get *had* by the takers and shakers of the world. I hope this is not going to be one of those scenarios. I just want to help them because suffering totally sucks. Veronica takes charge of herself and goes for a 2 hour massage with formal physiotherapy treatment. I find an albergue with Marcos where, of course, we run into friends: Tonni, the Germans, Roman and Pauli, and our Korean friends.

I see a guitar in the corner and the hospitalero begs me to play a song. She says she doesn't know how to play it, but she leaves it there in case someone will play for her. I am the first pilgrim to ever pick it up. I sing two songs for her before I am asked to shut up by a not-so-very-nice German man. I realize I have become this man's *Ukulele,* and I stutter a heartfelt Canadian apology.

Anyway, it's not like I burst into song at midnight. It is 6:00 pm. The hospitalero is beaming from ear to ear and thanking me profusely for making her day. Happy to oblige, Sugar!

I totally ignore the German fella, who really reminds me of somebody back home. Who, though? Which fun-sapping, rude curmudgeon is it? Is there a lesson here? My brain niggles and wiggles, but I just can't put my finger on it.

I have a nice dinner with Tonni, after a drink at the bar with friends. I laugh my head off all night. It seems like I have known Tonni for 20 years. He is such a nice man and I just want to hug him as proof that there are still nice men out there. The witty banter mixed with deep conversation is welcome for both of us. It almost feels like a date chalked up as a really

SELF-SACRIFICE AND EGO

wonderful platonic evening. I do not see Tonni again because in the morning, he is already gone. I'm sort of mad at the Camino for this.

CHAPTER 19

Boundaries

DAY 19 October 31

(Burgos to Hornillos del Carion 20 km /-)

This is one of the most important days of my Camino. As blissful as yesterday was, today's a disaster right off the Richter scale that shows me how much I still have to learn about boundaries. Further, I have things to let go of and I should take deep breaths when my patience is sorely tested.

To begin, Marcos is a doddler. He takes forever to pack but does share his breakfast so I feel roped in to waiting for him. It was a juicy orange that got me this time. I wanted to get going, but had reluctantly agreed to help him. I realize very early on in the day that the extra weight he wants me to carry is tanking me. It seemed so easy and light yesterday, but today it feels like a thousand pounds of rock.

Why the hell did I promise to help him?

What was it this time, Heather, pity? Or your big fat EGO?

I can't seem to get comfortable with my straps; my pack is digging into my hips and my flexors are screaming. I can't do this….but I made a promise. So I keep walking. We stop for a more substantial breakfast, after I foolishly assume he knows where we're going. After 30 minutes of being lost, I get pretty discouraged. Can't this guy at least NAVIGATE? I can barely walk my own pilgrimage, and now I'm trying to walk two people's Pilgrimages. I am the living hallmark of co-dependence right now and I'm irritated with myself for having no backbone.

I see Veronica and we say a tearful goodbye. I can feel her appreciation for my help yesterday, and I drink in this external validation a little too much. She gives me a pair of brand new socks as a *thank you*, which I don immediately. I wish I had gotten her contact information but even if I had, I would be a poor penpal with all of the Spanish I don't speak or write. I hug her hard, twice. I wish I were walking with her today instead of Marcos. I get the feeling that I've just messed up somehow, but wheels are already in motion and I'm evidently powerless to change the trajectory.

Marcos is eating super slowly. Does he think we are on a riverboat cruising down the Nile? It feels like he is taking his time on purpose but I don't know what his motive would be. I want to get out of Burgos so badly it's staining my attitude. He's just chewing and chewing his cud to smithereens, and I know deep in my marrow that he has got to be a reincarnation of my ex-husband. I regret helping out this chap who is enjoying being cared for while his steps are easy. How the heck am I going to get out of this? Boundary setting is an appallingly weak area for me.

When we're almost out of Burgos, I tell him I certainly won't be able to carry his things after today. Even as I say this, my Camino feels sabotaged. It feels sabotaged because I don't know if I can finish this Camino on my own steam without helping every "Tom, Dick and Harry". I explain that I am already having a lot of difficulty and he would literally have to be legally blind to think otherwise. He knows damn well that I'm suffering and he doesn't give a shit. Rather, he looks as though he is enjoying himself.

Is that a spring in his step?

Minutes later, I know I can't do a whole day like this, so I suggest going back into Burgos to get him a waist pack that might be easier on his back and hips. I think it's fair to set him up for success, after I made a promise I couldn't keep. Do I even owe him that? This right here is the kind of balderdash that sets women back a thousand years. I am a complete and utter pushover.

We take a bus back to the cathedral and wait for the sports store to open. He gets a pack, and I get ready to leave, but Marcos wants to keep shopping! My thoughts are turning murderous. "I have to get going", I tell him. Of course, he changes his mind about shopping and decides to come with me. Then, either to manipulate my time further or simply to annoy me, Marcos stops walking, while he's talking to me, every time he wants to make a point. This same quality that was so endearing in Jean Lou on our rest day in Puenta la Reina is a blatant manipulation of my time here in Burgos.

Steam might as well be coming out of my fucking ears.

I still have some of his things in my pack and it is so bloody heavy. It's starting to feel like I'm shouldering this man's sins. I agree to get him to the next town and then I'm giving him back his things for him to deal with. He keeps telling me he "just can't carry them", and begs me to keep carrying them for a bit longer. *Oh, this guy is good!* I'm going to go ahead and say he's masterful in the art of bull crap. He's somehow roping me into feeling sorry for him. Where in God's name is my backbone?! *Speak up Heather! Use your WORDS!*

The scenario is progressively worsening. He's saying things like, "You are just going to leave me, aren't you. You're just trying to get rid of me. I should trip you or something, so you hurt your knee and can't continue." *Ha! Ha! Joke. Joke.*

I am not laughing.

This guy is an eerie body double of my ex-husband. Dead weight, for sure. I'm also wondering if I might be in danger. We stop at the next town for a beer (... that I buy, because he's, "tight on cash"). I unload all of his things onto the tale. He looks grave. We have our parting beer and

I execute my escape. Alas, it is to no avail as he suddenly has renewed strength and decides to hike all afternoon with me.

Where are the other pilgrims?

HELP ME!

I have a better chance of winning the next lottery or populating Saturn than ditching this… this… calculating, bloody albatross! I can't even bring myself to talk to him anymore. I acknowledge that this is a reflection of my past and that this man before me is giving me a lesson. I try to be a good student. Perhaps I have a chance to create a better ending for my failed marriage today than I did back then. Maybe this is an opportunity; maybe this is the reason why Marcos is being so persistent. It would be nice to say a better goodbye to my ex-husband… But how?

What do I have to do?

What do I have to say?

My ex-husband wasn't a monster, but he was extremely dishonest about who he claimed to be. In the three years we dated, while I opened up about my whole life, he shovelled dirt over his. He could have told me his secrets but he chose not to, and it led to a laser-focused resentment on my part. We were already married by the time truth trickled in. It changed me. I felt trapped, and it made me hard and bitter. Because he lacked courage, or rather common-fucking-courtesy, it felt like he had stolen all of the sweetness out of me. My soul began to shrivel up, and eventually blew away. I walked around an empty shell for years afterwards.

He didn't like to work, which really burdened my life. I was always exhausted. I picked up more work to make ends meet. He had bills and child support that I felt obligated to pay on his behalf. He didn't bat an eye. He never said thank you. If anything, it made him more jealous, and that just made me feel resentful, bitter, and claustrophobic. Fighting became a daily event and crying myself to sleep every night became a part of the pattern. Eventually it became easier to acquiesce than to have yet another round of yelling. I learned to give in, in order to have temporary peace and quiet, and I think that's what burnt me out and led to my breast cancer. The stress was literally killing me.

Truth is, we still thought we loved each other. Dysfunction is hard to break free from. I liken it to having a horrible addiction. Pathetic as it is, I tried to stay as long as I could. I actually thought we would figure it out; that it would just take some time. We were both steeped in delusion by this point. I can't be the only divorcee in the world who has thought "did I do the right thing? Should I have stayed another 40 years?" To me, vows made during marriage were to God. I had a really hard time breaking those vows. I said I would stay married to this guy come what may, or some version of that.

The marriage was really hard to get over and I grieved the loss of what I thought we were and what could have been. I went through a brief catatonic-like depression, did lots of crying, and meditated the anger out of my vibrating cells. But that was a long time ago and I have forgiven him in my heart in the years past. Truly, I have. Whenever his name crosses my mind now, I send him love and kindness. I am so cheesy that I actually draw a heart in the air and push it outward. I hope his life is pleasant and that he is inwardly happy. It's all I've got, but I mean it.

I hope he can forgive me too, for my part. They say it takes two people to screw things up. I was a total and complete full-fledged bitch to him after discovering how much he had deceived me. Like I said, my sweetness had vanished. We ended the marriage with a rip and a tear, but maybe that was the only way to do it.

Perhaps there is a way to break free of my karma and old patterns. I pray to all the angels, saints, God, and all of the false Gods I can think of, and ask that they rise to my arsenal. *Come on and let's get this over with!*

Marcos and I hike and hike endlessly until we come across an Italian boy who is limping along. Fantastic, I have someone else to lavish my help on. Is this the only thing that soothes my ego? His English is pretty good and I ask him what the problem is. For his sprain, I leave my ankle brace with him that another traveller had given me in Puenta La Reina, and hike onward. Marcos and the Italian hike together and I take this opportunity to race ahead without a word. It is a brief salvation. Marcos is literally throwing rocks at me now. Why? Because he's an unstable madman, that's why! I turn and force a smile and say simply, "Buen Camino", and not any of the other things in my head.

Rocks!

Really?

Sheesh.

That's the thanks I get?

I'm outta here.

After 30 minutes of speed walking I hear steps behind me, and lo and behold, Marcos is trying to sneak up and scare me. I want to cry. *Fuck off! GET LOST! Leave me the fuck alone, crazy pants!* I scream in my head, but outwardly, I channel a smile from somewhere. Then he says to me, "Oh so you think you can get away just like that?"

What a creep!

There is nowhere to run and there is nowhere to hide. This situation could turn ugly fast, and I am walking on eggshells. I'm dusting this guy in the next town, Hornillos del Carion. I plan to carry on to Sambol, and I know he won't be able to do it. I'm late in the game for calculating but I have formulated an iron-clad plan.

> No one could solve my dilemma
> Nor could they tell me where I come from.
> Now, lost at the crossroads
> My heart bleeds, wondering
> Which way is home.
>
> –RUMI

As luck would have it, the Sambol albergue is closed at this time of year. It's 5:00 pm and I don't have enough daylight to get to Hontanas, which is 13 km away. I am just over-fucking-joyed to have to spend tonight with, essentially, my ex-husband embodied in Marcos at the moment. It gets better.

We have dinner.

My only respite is that I get to share the table with two Korean girls who don't really talk much, and their faces are impassive. What is going on here? I feel like I'm trapped in a bad dream that won't allow me to wake up. Anyway, let me just say it is good material for a sitcom, but I wish I wasn't the one starring in it. The conversation and my patience are frightfully strained, and I'm teetering on an emotional tight wire.

"Miss, more wine please."

After dinner, I try to find some time to write my thoughts down, but Marcos finds me and is trying to read over my shoulder. He is deliberately trying to distract me with talking and other outlandish, attention-seeking behaviour. *What are you, five years old? Can't you see I'm busy doing something?* I close my journal and get mocked by him for going to bed early.

My sleep was probably similar to having tetanus.

CHAPTER 20

Closure

DAY 20 November 01

(Hornillos del Camino to Itero de la Vega 39km then to Boadilla)

I get up super-duper early to pack and eat. Marcos catches me before I can sneak away. He's doing his doddling though, so I know he won't be leaving any time soon. I give him my most sincere hug and I actually mean it. My last words are "Keep going on your Camino. Don't be too hard on yourself". I know it wasn't much to offer, but it really did make for a better ending.

I turn and leave the albergue like Satan's on my ass. Relief isn't a big enough word to describe this moment. About 2 km out of town I need to go to the bathroom… emergently. I find a grassy knoll to do my business, and I hope with the thick fog that no one will see me. I vacate the largest number 2 of my lifetime. It's one of those ones… that you just can't wipe enough away, and I've used ridiculous amounts of toilet paper to get the job done right. I stand back and realize that I cannot leave things as they are, so I search for a large stone and place the craggy rock over the entire mess. I stand back to admire my work. I have in every sense, metaphorically and physically, sepulchred my shit. I feel dizzy and giddy because I'm finally free. "Goodbye, David!" I say out loud for no one to hear.

In the concealment of the fog, I light a cigarette and walk away.

Around 11:30 am, I run into my trail daughters from Korea. I get hugs and kisses. One of the girls is sad because she has lost Sam (USA), whom she has a crush on. He has travelled on ahead. I encourage her to walk her own Camino and allow him the freedom to walk his. I buy us girls some Coca-Cola and we sit outside in the sunshine talking out our thoughts. I feel like a trail mom and it feels kind of nice. Never having had children of my own, I'm happy to be their substitute mom for a time. I could never hack the real thing and I know it.

As we walk together into the next small village, we spot Sam in the street. I thank him again for the egg he gave me and he just shrugs his shoulders. "No biggie Heather, I found it in the fridge and no one claimed it. It was free." Here I was all worked up over inequality and the universe was just trying to give me an egg for breakfast. A round of hugs and a bit of chatting ensues, but I know that the girls have some decisions to make. I walk on and leave them to it. Love can be difficult at any age, but like trout gumming for a shiny lure, we always go for it despite the risk.

It's the human condition.

I power walk on to Itero, but the town feels strange to me. I don't want to stay here and I can't really explain why. I stop at a bar for a coffee with some cognac to thaw my freezing fingers and toes. The men in the bar ogle and seem creepy. Am I being paranoid now? Regardless, it's time to move on to Boadilla. I feel like I got out just in time. I climb a hill with a 1500 meter ascent to find a large message board at the top with a nearby picnic area. It is about 2 pm, so I break for lunch and to read a few of the messages. I leave a message for the Korean girls and for Sam congratulating them on their progress in life and on the Camino. Surprised, I find one for me from Roberto wishing me a buen Camino and telling me he missed me. It's so nice to be thought of, and moreover, to have someone believe I could make it this far. The message was dated for yesterday, which means he is a full day ahead of me. Perhaps we will have a reunion in the next couple of days. That would be wonderful because I could really use the mental lift.

The Meseta is the part of the trail that is said to represent the mind. It is where a lot of pilgrims have their greatest difficulty. The mind can be a murky place to dwell for any of us at any time and it is so important to keep up our hope. Someone once told me that "we don't have to believe our thoughts, nor do we have to feel them!" That is so true, but sometimes, this is easier said than done.

My obvious downfall was the first third of the trail, which is linked to the physical. The Meseta, however, nearly drove me into madness dealing with my pseudo ex-husband. Physically, I feel stronger and more powerful with the first third of the trail completed. I cross my fingers hoping that I have passed my Meseta test. I would be awfully nice to walk unperturbed for a little while. I feel as though I'm getting some good stuff worked out here and I am pleased with this progress. At the moment, it seems like things are really turning around for me.

There is a delicious simplicity to walking. All you have to do is put one foot in front of the other and move forward. There are no calls or emails to return, no errands to run, no work or other demands on my schedule. I'm free. My schedule is simply walking, eating, and sleeping; albeit, with no amenities. I have time to re-order my thoughts and explore them if I choose. There is plenty of time to think and not to think while I breathe and listen to my breath. I experience everything and nothing.

The click of my walking sticks soothes, and they are my companions. I am deliberately re-calibrating with intention; it has been a worthwhile journey into myself. The Camino is the hardest task I have ever embarked upon; however, it is the kindest gesture I have given myself thus far. That sentence is a mouthful, but it couldn't be more, true.

I have been following a Spaniard from Ibiza, the Island south of Mallorca, all day. He has also travelled 39 km today. We reach an albergue at the same time. We enter and I see a young Frenchman who had been hiking, until now, with his girlfriend. There is no sign of the girlfriend. They had been travelling together for weeks, and he tells me that 2 days ago he expressed a need to hike alone. Apparently his girlfriend is ahead in the next town. Follow up questions don't seem necessary. I've seen many couples separate for a time along The Way. The Camino is wreaking havoc on everyone.

There are no shortcuts, no stones unturned, no ghosts un-dealt with, and no respite from the dreams. How could I ever explain the Camino experience to anyone without risking institutionalization? I can't even articulate what's happening to me. This experience has been a giant mirror showing me myself: the good, the bad, and the ugly.

At times, I have been utterly helpless in my suffering here on this walk and in my life back home. Yet, in the next moment, I'll be overwhelmed with joy over the littlest thing. I've had to improvise and accept altered endings. I'm assuming there is a plan for me after this trail is done, even if it isn't by my own design. I can't help but see my ego on a platter before me and I am troubled by my own stupidity. Apparently I need daily ass-kicking reminders to keep me on track. I needed this Camino havoc to reboot my hard drive. I may very well become a butterfly after all of this fucking metamorphosis.

I had to see myself first before I could truly experience God. Self-awareness is a chore. I have tried my best to forgive myself for the mistakes I've made that have contaminated my life. With some of that tidied up, I thought I'd better go ahead and forgive God, whom I thought had abandoned me, in order to feel the forgiveness He had been giving me all along.

Done. Done.

And done.

I guess I want to see this Compostela through for both God and myself. And now, today, I feel strangely re-energized enough to believe He wants me to do it too!

CHAPTER 21

More Dreams

DAY 21 November 02

(Boadilla to Carrion de los Condes 26 - 28km)

I dreamed about my first-ever boyfriend last night. We dated throughout high school before I broke up with him and broke his heart. I broke my own heart too but I was too young to explain the pressure I was experiencing at home to him; the abuse I had endured and restlessness within me to run and run until I could run no more. He was a steady young man, and a good man. He was the kind of guy that was destined to build life on a solid foundation. He was exactly what I needed, but I felt I had to work out my problems and heal myself on my own, before I could be any good to him.

As a teenager, I really didn't have the vocabulary to say all of this and I hadn't realized yet what was really bothering me. I have always felt awful that I hurt him and never got the chance to explain why. Now that I think about it, I never actually saw him again after high school. When we were dating, we both loved running, and we got along very peacefully. He was the perfect gentle boyfriend and he made me laugh every day. His life dream was to live in a small cabin together in a small town up north someday; the life I am living now, twenty years later. Back then, I only wanted to be free and to travel. This was the beginning of a landslide and I broke it all apart by cheating on him. I don't know if he ever knew, and I didn't have the courage to tell him. I have regretted my weak moment for all these years, but I have at least made sure to never make same mistake again.

Mistakes like that haunt a person.

In the dream, I tell him what I had done with my head hung in shame. I can't look up at him. He shrugs his shoulders and says, "We were young. It doesn't matter now. Know that I loved you so much, Heather." He shows me his wedding band and says to me he can do nothing about this now. He hugs me hard and I fall into his embrace. I am forgiven. When I awake in the morning it is the first time in 22 years that I feel unburdened by guilt. Our souls were able to speak last night in the spirit of healing. I can finally let it go now. This Camino is a strange and beautiful animal.

Facing my own darkness and my black book of ghosts, one by one has been a difficult challenge. No one wants to look at themselves in a less than glamorous light, but I know that I feel better about myself now that I'm sorting through all of my pieces. I have more healing work to do; so many painful memories buried deep within my core. Maybe my broken pieces will become a pretty mosaic someday; something I can be proud of.

I'm getting good at packing quickly, and I start hiking at 7:20 am. My goal is 46 km today. A lofty goal, I realize, but yesterday went so well, so I figure I should go while the going is good. I hike the first 6 km without food or water, and I am famished when I get to Fromista. The problem is the strong wind force again. Though I am hiking very fast, my energy is draining due to the elements. It's hard to keep walking in a straight line and I have to concentrate on the road before me. In Fromista, I eat two breakfasts and two coffees. The waitress looks at me oddly, but I pay her no attention. I could have eaten more, but how do you order three breakfasts and maintain any self-respect?

The conditions worsen throughout the day, and now it's raining with no shelter in sight. It would be suicide to try to stop and put my backpack cover on in these winds. It's one foot in front of the other until I stop, exhausted, at 26 km in Carrion de los Condes. I don't think that I looked up once.

Must get to shelter has been the only mantra playing in my head.

My muscles are screaming. I walk into the first place I see and take off my pack, jacket, mitts, etc., but get the impression the staff aren't into Peregrinos. This happens occasionally. I put all of my wet things back on and head out a little nonplussed. I'm wondering what to do or where to go next, since it's a holiday. Things seem to happen for a reason, and such as it is this time. The very moment I leave the bar, I see Tonni, Sarah, and Mike emerge across the street. They tell me where their albergue is and to go straight there. They are all headed to the store to get food for tonight. I do what I am told and forfeit my goal of 46 km like a hot potato. I ask Tonni what he is doing here still because I thought he had been heading back home to Denmark, but don't get an immediate answer. Questions fill my head but I change the subject. He looks as though he has a lot on his mind at the moment.

I tell Tonni I learned a big lesson in Burgos, but unfortunately, there's no time to talk yet. I check into what I would consider to be a 5-star albergue run by nuns. It's clean, large, there are *beds*, hot water, and lights that stay on while showering!

It's Shangri-La… in some ways.

By the time I shower and grab a bite to eat, it's time for mass. We go as a pilgrim group. This is the first time I don't cry in church, and come to think of it, this is the first time the priest doesn't shake our hands. *Hm, is that significant? Am I more healed?* Aurie invites me to a French movie with Spanish subtitles. He laughs at his own joke because he knows I can't speak either language. I laugh too, but graciously decline. I settle into my bed at 10 pm and my last visual is a Portuguese fellow full-frontal flashing me. I pull my toque down over my eyes.

CHAPTER 22

Chemotherapy?

```
DAY 22 November 03
(Carrion de los Condes to Sahagun 42 km)
```

The morning is sort of the same. Mr. naked-Portuguese-man is using his laptop while posing in both sitting and standing positions, with a crazy-ass smile on his face. I deliberately avoid looking in his direction. I'm not going to encourage this lunatic's behaviour. A pilgrim in the next bed to mine tells me "he bicycled his legs in the air last night. Lying in bed. With no underwear on, for a really, really long time." I bust up laughing. Really? Because *any* amount of time is too much time to "air bicycle with no underwear on". That's a classic! I'm almost sad I missed it.

Dorm life is certainly starting to have its drawbacks. Did I mention the albergue was run by nuns? What would the nuns think about Mr. naked-Portuguese-man splashing his manhood around at the bathroom sink this morning? So maybe it isn't Shangri-La for that reason, and I gather the nuns will have to sanitize this whole area with twice-blessed Holy water.

Mike and Tonni like to journal all of their thoughts in the morning, so Sarah and I hit the trail. We don't get very far. The nearest bar is a stone's throw away and we stop for café con leche. Something about the morning coffee is not only a social event but also a pilgrim's liquid pep talk. It's a soul vitamin. It's a cup of courage, really.

The group soon joins us. I feel great today and slept amazingly. I feel no pain at all, which is a modern day miracle. I think this is all possible because my feet have either denervated themselves or managed to develop a hardy form of scar tissue. I really don't have spectacular feeling to my great toes. Is that reason for concern? Whatever the reason, I am tickled pink that it's comfortable to walk again.

Mike shares with the group that he's walking the Camino to decide whether or not he would like to become a priest. We are all taken by surprise, possibly because he doesn't *look* like a priest? Mike is an easy smiling, broad-shouldered, tall, groomed, blond-haired, blue eyed, good looking fellow who's *maybe* in his late twenties or early thirties. He looks *varsity*, he looks preppy and yacht-ready. I can't even picture him in robes, but I am *now*. Mike the Priest. Well that's wonderful! We lean in and ask for more details. He is a mite reticent, but still smiling. It's personal and we lean back into our chairs in one motion. I can't help but think *dentist*, now.

I give him my email address because I want to hear about his journey in life; whatever he chooses to do, he will be phenomenal. He beams at all of us, but I sense the gravity of his decision by the brief shadow that passes his eyes. Does doubt penetrate all of us… even the Holy?

The first 17 km is gale force winds and rain. There is nothing but farmer's fields for miles. Regardless, I happen to love the Meseta these days. I feel strong and I don't even mind the monotonous landscape. The sound of my breath and the crunch of my steps lilt me along in a meditative rhythm.

Sarah and I have a pretty incredible conversation at the start of the hike. I tell her about Burgos and what happened with my pseudo ex-husband, and she tells me she understands since she had met her pseudo brother in a similar fashion. *Oh good*, I don't feel nearly as crazy now. She tells me she's walking the Camino for her brother, who is addicted to drugs. A once sweet, loving, and helpful person has become disconnected from himself. She explains his behaviours now include lying, disappearing, and stealing from the family. All of the interventions they've tried and efforts they've made have failed to restore him.

Personally, she has experienced stress in the form of weight loss, job struggles, and a lot of anxiety. On the trail, she met a pilgrim who had eyes that resembled her brother's. She immediately recognized a similar dynamic with this pilgrim that she has with her brother. She explains that it took her two days to shake the guy loose. I tell her I had a similar experience and now that it's over, I'm strangely grateful for having had it.

I move past Sarah after a time, and hike alone for a few hours. The solace is healing. I stop in a town to rest, and Mike (USA) catches up with me. Aurie, Sarah, and Tonni start trickling in, and we have lunch together. The Czech fellows, Pauli and Roman, are there too, and it's a grand ol' reunion. I order a tortilla slice (quiche) to fortify and end up hiking 42 km that day. I feel like a million dollars.

The last 13 km is a power-hike with a Basque Spanish man about 20 years my senior. We are absolutely race-walking. I'm stunned by how strong and fast he is for his age. I'm stunned at how strong and fast I am for *my* age. Compared to only few days ago, I am no longer the world's worst pilgrim. I feel like my old self again, and I'm so happy to see the athlete within emerge.

I ask this lean powerhouse his name after a time, and with a sun-glinted toothy grin, he tells me his name is Santiago. I have to pick my jaw up from the ground. This man just hiked me into Sahagun at a champion pace. I have renewed hope that I will reach my final destination. Since his name, Santiago, is my destination, I take it to be a sign of cosmic blessing.

Victory doesn't last long. At dinner, I feel nauseated and feverish at the restaurant, which forces me to leave early. It isn't long before I am projectile vomiting with a side order of explosive diarrhea. I am fantastically ill with a high fever, aches and chills, and I think I may need medical attention. I soil my underwear so thoroughly that I have to toss them away into the only garbage can… which just so happens to be in the kitchen. I get about 5 minutes of sleep, curled up on the concrete bathroom floor hugging the toilet. I'm so cold my teeth are chattering. A thought flits through my mind that this might be the Camino's way of re-enacting my chemotherapy experience.

On the other hand, I could just have a flu bug.

CHAPTER 23

Whisper of Thanks

DAY 23 November 04

(Sahagun to Bercianos 10km)

I have to make some decisions. I'm in no condition to get out of bed, but if I stay here, I will freeze solid. I take the 2 Imodium tablets I have in my stores and pack up my stuff.

It's cold and pouring rain outside. I am still shitting to beat the band and washed over green with nausea. I can't pretend that I added much value to the breakfast conversation, but Tonni and Mike are valiant gents who dared to sit with me, the plagued. They have both been wonderful to help me through this. Mike brought things to help me when I was prostrated on the bathroom floor, and now Tonni is carrying my backpack on his front. They are committed to getting me to the next town, which is 10.5 km away. I sob silently the whole way there. I can't help it. I ache all over and I can hardly move forward. I don't say a word the entire way for fear of shitting myself or puking again. I have only my hiking poles to carry and they are nearly too much for me to manage. The men really took charge and helped me over this hurdle. My thank you comes out in a whisper.

Tonni finds an albergue at a quaint home in Bercianos. The hospitaleros jump into action and treat me like their child; though our ages may have been similar. I am put to bed, and Tonni stays with me instead of hiking on. He does my laundry while I sleep for 5 hours. When I wake I am given a shot of something like Schnapps, a cup of tea, and water to wash down lentil stew. Feels like heaven. Tonni wraps a blanket around me at the kitchen table and the senora lights the wood stove. I want to move in and stay forever. I am overwhelmed by the love I'm receiving and I'm too sick to reject anything.

Tonni wants to come back someday and help them build an addition onto the house, which would add 20 beds for weary pilgrims. This guy has a big, soft, gooey heart. He has his own construction company in Denmark and thinks he may donate about 10 days to these people. A generous offer, and I suspect he really will come back to do it. I'm proud of him. This guy is the real deal. It makes me think back to my mission work in Belize in 2006. Selfless acts of charity always yield more for yourself than what you give. At the moment, I have nothing at all to give.

The hospitalero's husband is outside walking their goat on a leash. It's worth mentioning because this isn't something I had ever seen before. Of course, I may have been hallucinating.

By now, the albergue is full and I am the only female pilgrim. I am getting the Princess treatment, which is good practice for someone in need of learning how to receive. I'm too weak to protest. The universe is literally forcing its hand while Kevin's words echo back to me about being tender and loving to myself.

I am glad that I have a friend with me today. I really wasn't coping well earlier. Tonni could have easily ditched me and hiked onward, which is probably what he should have done. I would not at all have been upset with him. I worry that I have ruined his plans to be in Leon by Monday, where he means to leave for Denmark. He had taken the time off to do the entire pilgrimage but realized that he wanted to finish it with his son one day. He explains that doing the Camino with his son will bring him greater fulfillment than completing it on his own.

When I get up five hours later, I take the hottest and longest shower of my Camino. I have NEW soap and it's exciting. I even have time to shave my legs and armpits; which is kind of nice. I don't want the goat to think I'm grass.

I'm sitting in the living room in a big comfy chair by the fire when I realize that the albergue is actually this couple's private home. The only room that is off limits is their bedroom. No wonder it feels like home. I still feel awful but at least I'm resting and warm. Honestly, if it were Tonni that was ill I would tell him to stay in bed for days. But I know I will hike on tomorrow. Stubborn woman, stubborn nurse! Dinner is lively and completely in Spanish. Again, I'm happy to have Tonni around to talk with. He's a 6'4 Danish gentle giant, who just happens to speak very good English.

CHAPTER 24

The Camino Provides

DAY 24 November 05 Sunday

(Bercianos to Mansilla de las Mulas 26km)

Except for stabbing abdominal pain and diarrhea, I feel pretty good. I have no appetite, but I eat a yogurt and some cereal because I know I should. I add more money to the donativo box because this home has been so restorative. I take a picture with Rosa, the lady of the house, to mark the memory, and I thank her profusely for her love and kindness. Rosa has hiked the Camino four times and her Compostela certificates are hanging in display over the stove. I gaze respectfully at her framed miracles. She and her husband have since opened their home as an albergue because they feel they understand what pilgrims need most. She's right. They were an ace in my hand and it made all the difference in getting me back on the trail.

The first 4 hours of hiking is straight, flat farmland, without a tree in sight, which is fantastic for people with diarrhea. Tonni keeps asking me if I'm going for a number 1 or a number 2. I tell him, "Shut up you big foolish Dane". He replies, "Okay, Princess, but you have to use hand sanitizer when you get back from behind that blade of grass". He has jugs of this stuff in his bag.

We stop at the one and only empty Spanish town to rest and meet up with Pauli and Roman. Pauli has a touch of what I have; it's been going around. Roman is no better with his head cold. We are a good looking bunch. Pauli and I wonder if there was a bad *water fuente* yesterday, and we figure out that we filled our bottles at the same fountain. Is this water contamination that has felled us, or a terrible flu bug? Either way, I know privately that my lesson here is reviewing my time during cancer treatment. Did it ever occur to God that I've hardly forgotten it? I order a banana and a beer for lunch; you couldn't *pay* me to drink the water anymore!

The next and last 6 km are brutal. My stomach is rock hard and distended to the point of explosion. I feel like I might rip apart, my guts spilling all over the ground. The pain is blinding. I have to stop several times to get my bearings and I end up just lying down on the road. The other pilgrims are long gone by now and I'm alone, flat on my back, blinking up at the sky. It feels like someone has hit the pause button; it's an eerily similar feeling to when I was full on battling cancer. I check my wrist and feel my pulse flutter. I'm having more irregular heartbeats than usual, and I wonder how bad my electrolyte imbalance is. I either need a shovel to bury my own body, or a taxi and some Gatorade.

I need to somehow get up off the street. I whisper to God, "Help".

I sit upright. The town is about 2 km away but it's an inch at a time. I see Roman walking back towards me. Oh my God! Thank *God*! For the second time in 2 days my pack is lifted from my shoulders and carried for me. I don't have enough salt to cry.

Where would I be without all of these Trail Angels? I think back to Marcos, and I remember an angry flippant thought, "I would never resort to this and have someone carry my pack". And so, my good deed has been twice repaid and in as many days. I see that I'm still working on my ego.

I fall into bed in Manzanilla and I am covered with blankets by some kind soul at the albergue. Only my head is visible. Pauli makes me tea and the hospitalero brings me an electrolyte drink. Huh. The trail or *something* always provides!

I am feverish, but I feel like I might already be improving. A large space heater is brought into my room but I just can't seem to get warm. I sleep for hours upon end. The hospitalero tells me I must stay for a few days to rest, and not to eat anything unless my body asks for it. She suggests rice or something, but no milk. "Thanks, Mom." If my fever is better tomorrow, I may still try to get to Leon. It's a bigger city so I pray they have a pharmacy and a store that sells replacement bodies. I'm not sure if I'm being practical or just plain stubborn. The point it is, I can't stay here. There is no medicine, food, or bottled water for miles.

One thing I've learned in my life is that calamity, along with it's cousin, disaster, can end up being the best thing in the long run. Positive change always comes out of it; or shall I say, there is great potential for positive change. There is nothing like calamity and disaster to get the attention of humans who are on the wrong track. It's the old celestial clunk on the head. I am certifiably clunked right now. I am awake and listening.

Hello?

HELLO?

In the meantime, I will rest while the others go out and explore the ghost town. I'm pleased as punch to have my glass of electrolytes, and at the moment, it's as filling as a steak dinner. I am TLC'ing this whole scenario right now. I get it. Slow down and start enjoying the moment. I'm still chewing on what that is going to look like. My pride is taking a hard hit, along with my body. *Am I done walking?*
Is the show over? Did I fail?
Sarah is also at this albergue, so we share a room. We had lost her a few days back, but she was able to catch up to us, seeing as we had a really short day, yesterday. It is so great to see her. She's ailing with a few issues of her own. I give her what medicines I have that suit her conditions, but for anything more she'll have to find a pharmacy. The Camino is a trail, not a destination. It is a pathway to somewhere else with the implied suggestion that one keep movin' on. Staying put would merely prolong the agony. We are meant to deal with our suffering, not wallow in it.

THE PILGRIM'S STONE

Me

After a full day of climbing up and down the Pyronees mountains, I came across this daunting sign. So, just for fun I want you to picture in your mind's eye, the look on my face. Yup! That's about right!

Roberto. Picnic by the river.

THE CAMINO PROVIDES

Pyronees.

Thomas.

All I can say is wet, rain and sandals.

THE PILGRIM'S STONE

Jean Lou

THE CAMINO PROVIDES

I must remember to thank Columbia for making sturdy sandals.

The World in a display of stones.

My Welsh Posse in Puenta La Reina.

Fuente del Vino.

Trail Angels

THE CAMINO PROVIDES

Wooden Crosses

THE PILGRIM'S STONE

The beginning of burden in Burgos.

Leaving my past behind.

THE CAMINO PROVIDES

Mike, Myself, Sarah, Stephan, and Tonni.

Rosa, Myself, Tonni and other Spansh Pilgrims outside of Sahagun.

Sarah, Roman, and Pauli.

THE PILGRIM'S STONE

Sahagun Alburgue.

Cruz de Ferro.

Soul Sisters.

THE CAMINO PROVIDES

Astorga.

Rabanal.

Cruz de Ferro.

El Acebo.

Castle in Ponferrada

THE CAMINO PROVIDES

Orphaned.

Solitude.

Same trail. New beginning.

Myself and Gerhild.

THE PILGRIM'S STONE

The stick carrying a boulder.

Flavio, Hilde and Chris.

Veronica and I.

THE CAMINO PROVIDES

The image of Tranquility.

Flavio 'the Great'

Just another day on the Way.

THE PILGRIM'S STONE

Bliss.

A trail marker indicating only 20km left to go until I reach Santiago. A lot of thoughts are crossing my mind at this moment.

Arrival to Santiago.

Pilgrim Party on the Boulevard. These pilgrim's had been cheering for other Pilgrims arriving to Santiago for 3 straight hours.

THE CAMINO PROVIDES

Saying thank-you to my feet for their service to me.

Victory pose.

Finisterre – The end of the World. Gerhild and I.

The last Tamoxifen pill I will ever take before releasing my Cancer journey to the fire.

THE PILGRIM'S STONE

Our ceremonial Fire included a sip of wine that felt a lot like communion.

Feet that walked a long way in gratitude.

THE CAMINO PROVIDES

Pilgrim's in Santiago.

A final goodbye to Gerhild before heading home.

SOUL

(Leon to Santiago)

> "When you are full of joy, you move faster and you want to go about doing good to everyone. 'Joy is the sign of union of God' – of God's presence."
>
> –Mother Teresa

Section 3 -

SOUL: The soul aspect of the pilgrimage begins in the last third of the Camino. It is a time of unburdening sin through forgiveness by God and of ourselves, with a spiritual awakening that brings joyful bliss and fulfillment. It is an earned step, and the universal acknowledgement is a feeling of lightness and well being.

CHAPTER 25

I Am a Pilgrim, Not a Hiker

DAY 25 November 06

(Mansilla to Leon 18km +/-)

My plan was to go 9 km past Leon to keep on track with my asinine plan of hiking the whole way to Santiago by the 17th of November. I wake feeling fairly rested and just plain happy I haven't shit the bed for a few days. If there was ever a scale with which to judge one's progress, I suggest starting there. Fatigue is still my constant companion and I believe it lingers only to remind me I'm alive. I make a rice pudding with apples and cinnamon topped with sugar, for breakfast. It attracts pilgrims like flies to honey, which makes me happy to be able to give back a little. Food feels pretty good in the belly for a change.

I need to do a little self-evaluation here. It isn't right that other people are carrying my backpack. I don't know if my body can do this anymore. It's been one thing after another. I want to quit and go home. *Today.* I'm the definition of depleted. I give myself the spiel about love and tenderness toward myself. I haven't exactly been following my own advice. At this point, everyone has hiked on past me, and though I feel lonely for the first time, I'm proud of them for following their own paths. I don't want anyone to feel anchored to me. These are my issues and I have to master them on my own. The reality for me right now though is a large helping of misery; plain and simple.

What?

Did I hear my name?

Pauli is hailing me in for a coffee where Roman and Sarah are waiting. Every time I've faced difficulty on this journey, I've been given an emotional lift when I needed it most. I'm so happy to see everyone. It looks like I haven't been left behind after all.

We take some group photos, talk, and rest. My stomach just won't settle down, and I spend a good ten minutes destroying the bathroom. It's a classy scene. I need a pharmacy, a doctor, and a shaman! Lucky for me there's at least a pharmacy nearby, so I load up on Imodium, Compeed foot care, and sunblock for my lips. The lip balm is a special treat since my lips are starting to look like chapped toes. I'm a trail goddess inside and out!

Sarah and I walk the rest of the way into Leon together, but 3 km out we both have to stop. We get some tea and sit outside. I tell her I'm considering taking a bus tomorrow. It's the first time I've said it out loud and it sounds like defeat. She tells me, "I'm glad you're saying this. You were so focused on the kilometres, and your body is telling you something else". I guess I had wanted to be a hiker and a pilgrim. Sarah is also feeling unwell, so I may have myself a bus companion. I'm not even sure that companionship would lessen the blow. All I know is I've been fooling myself for a while now and enough is enough.

I could start by clipping 40 km by bus to give myself a day of rest and some extra time in Finisterre. I've decided that's where I want to take my last Tamoxifen pill before I set the bottle and the rest of the pills on fire. That's all I know for sure at the moment. With my mind set on the decision to take a bus, I feel at ease. My goals are changing so rapidly. My

I AM A PILGRIM, NOT A HIKER

Camino has been a rollercoaster, but now I just want to tidy things up and see Spain. I'm done with the physical and mental. It's time for soul. I have the notion that everything will get done perfectly; a blended harmony of body, mind and soul.

I like Leon! I check in with Sarah and surprise her with matching bracelets. She tells me she has few close girlfriends and is grateful for my friendship. We make tentative plans for a Camino reunion somewhere in the future. I love the idea!

While Sarah goes for a shower, I go for a beer with Ingrid, a newbie from Belgium. We have quite a conversation. Ingrid is a fresh faced, inwardly strong, and sweet woman. She is 49 and has 2 grown children, but her husband and mother have both died in recent years. She is struggling with her grief and finding the courage to live again. I try to put myself in her shoes and wonder how hard that kind of grief is. Death hasn't affected my life in any major way yet, so I empathize the best way I can.

Her struggle is a far more difficult one than mine. She has hiked from Sarria to Santiago and feels like she has had her Camino. She's going home tomorrow because she has received what she needed from the trail". The certainty in her voice is inspiring. I "got" my Camino in Los Arcos, but still I feel compelled to move forward. How does she know with so much certainty there is nothing left for her here? I revere her strength, and I tell her so.

The bar closes at 4:00 pm, so Ingrid and I part with well wishes. I do my duty of showering my body while doing laundry at the same time. I use the same soap to scrub everything. It's been so cold and damp that nothing dries completely overnight. Damp underwear is especially nice, but wet socks are a close second. There have been days I simply can't bear it, so I turn everything inside out for a laundry holiday. Clean travel standards are nonexistent. I walked past a *perfumeria* earlier and it stopped me dead in my tracks. It was like looking through the glass at some other world to which I once belonged, but no longer really do.

Except for Sarah, everyone thinks I've hiked onward. It's a surprise and a real celebration when I turn up at the bar and all of my trail friends are there. Tonni asks me what happened, and I explain that my body is shutting down, and it's important for me to put the kilometres aside and focus on the spiritual for the remainder of my time. It made no sense to hike 9 km more and be alone for dinner when all of my friends were in Leon. I want to enjoy every moment now. He understands completely, adding he has done the same thing before. I wonder if he might be talking about me.

I am really looking forward to seeing the Cruz de Ferro, walking the last 100 km and seeing Santiago. I will have to budget my time, stay healthy, and bus what I have to. I want to spend my time in blissful meditation and reflection. Does God have anything more to say to me? I will keep my ears to my heart and soul from here on out. This has been a hard decision to make; a tearful one actually, but I feel a lot lighter now that I've made it, and I know I have made the right decision.

I had purchased fridge magnets that say Leon for my friends. I pass them out and they squeal like children. It's such a small memento, but it is my gesture of gratitude to say thanks for all the help and good times. We are a group of 10 tonight, and we eat and drink to our hearts' content. It's the first real meal I've had in days; I take it slowly. *Gurgle. Gurgle.* I look down the table at each face, and drink in deeply the atmosphere of tender loving friendship.

Tonni pleasantly surprises us by paying the entire tab. This is his gesture of thanks to all of us. He tells me quietly it is not for ego that he pays the bill, but simply because he is in a good position in life to do so. Therefore, he felt he should. It was really a lovely way to spend an evening. We race back to the albergue because the gates close sharply at 9:30 pm. We've met pilgrims who have missed curfew and have been left out in the cold without their packs or sleeping bags. I shudder to imagine what that would be like.

We're immediately shuffled off to church by the hospitalero. Our albergue is a monastery, and the nuns want to see us. We obediently go. Of course, I forget my glasses but one of the nuns sees me struggling and produces my exact prescription from her pocket. A pilgrim should never fear because everything is provided when it is really needed. That's the difference between our *wants* and our *needs*. I make a mental note to look for more miracles in my life when I get home. I hear they are all around us if we choose to notice them.

I AM A PILGRIM, NOT A HIKER

> Troubled by questions all my life,
> Like a madman I have been
> knocking at the door.
> It opened!
> I had been knocking from inside.
>
> –RUMI

The nun speaks to us before we enter the church. She tells us the importance of being a pilgrim and how being on The Way is meant to bring us closer to God; to find God. Looking directly into my eyes, she tells us in Spanish, "We are not hikers, we are pilgrims!" A tingle travels up my spine. It confirms my decision earlier today to embrace the spiritual aspect of my pilgrimage. I'm at a loss for words, which is fine because we're shuffled forward into the church. As we enter from the back, the nuns enter from the front. They begin to sing in a way that I've never before had the pleasure of hearing. The notes float over us, surround us, and lift us. It is the most incredible thing I have ever witnessed. I begin to cry because the music moves me so much. It is ethereal perfection. These women, these nuns, *seem so holy.*

The nun who spoke to us earlier tells us to ask ourselves why we are pilgrims. Why are we here? Where are we going? And why? I don't have the answers to any of these questions. While I listen to the sisters breathe sounds not humanly possible, I have to wonder how fortunate I am to be here in this exact moment. How is it that I'm even alive?

I'm so choked up I can barely speak afterwards. I'm still savouring the music when I hear my name being called by Tonni. He wishes me a good night in a tone that has an ocean of sadness to it. All I want to do is collapse into his arms and rest my face on his, but I just give him a quick hug and say goodnight. My heart is breaking. He is leaving tomorrow regardless of how I feel, and more time would have only made things harder in the end. I know I will never see him again but there is the palest solace in knowing perhaps our hearts understand one another. I absolutely adore the guy and I sure will miss my friend when he's gone. Tonni's purpose for me has been a restoration of faith that there is a sweetheart out there for me; preferably in Canada. There have been quite a few good guys along the Way: Pauli, Roman, Daniel, Sam, Roberto, Mike, and Thomas, to name a few.

Focus on the positive, Heather!

This is really not an effort to disparage Grizzly, because he has his good qualities; emotional intimacy just isn't one of them. All I know for sure is he isn't the one for me and I am not the right one for him either. I mentally try blessing the whole situation by saying that I hope we both find the right love for each of us, but with other people. It doesn't hurt any less with this declaration. I need to meet someone who doesn't keep secrets. It makes me batshit crazy; it makes ALL women bat-shit crazy. We all lack common sense when it comes to love; whether it's a good love or a bad one, you love who you love, and that's that.

Sarah gives me a tiny ring and a bracelet. She has included a written postcard that makes me laugh. It is a good memory of our day together and the decisions we've both made. I tuck the postcard into my diary for safekeeping. I go to bed thinking about Tonni and the lesson he's taught me. *Farewell, Tonni.* I drift off into a dreamless sleep.

CHAPTER 26

Orphaned

DAY 26 November 07

(475 km in the bag Leon to Astorga to Rabanal)

I see Teracilla from Italy. She's the lady I met in Pamplona who had broken her wrist. Today I find her wrapping up her ankle. I ask her how her head is, because maybe she has injured that, as well? She gets my joke and laughs with me about her clumsiness. It's great to see her after such a long time.

Sarah is already packed up and ready to go. She has decided to walk instead of taking a bus. She thinks it will be better for her to have time alone to think. I applaud her insightfulness and am deeply proud of her.

The group is splitting up today and the air is heavy because of it. I see Tonni, and we can barely look at one another. He gives me his hand sanitizer and some Ibuprofen. He keeps the roll of duct tape I give him. We meet for breakfast. I can only take tea. His arm is resting beside mine, touching, and it feels good and warm. I'm barely holding up in my corner.

We say goodbye with a hug, and he starts crying too. It feels like a rip and a tear when we turn away from each other. Totally platonic and yet unexplainably intimate. Sarah, Roman, Pauli, and Tonni are all departing in different directions. I sit in the courtyard and bawl my eyes out beside a beautiful garden. Pigeons coo at my feet in an effort to calm me. I walk away in some direction. I don't even know where I'm going, and have no clue where the bus station is.

I stop in a café to rest and write until I am pulled together. I am still a pilgrim, but I feel like an orphan. Doing a Camino solo is anything but solo. The people I've met have changed everything. They have supported me and shown me love and understanding. We've had countless laughs together under an umbrella of multicultural finesse. We are all seekers and we have shared our insights, unabashedly. I have made some impactful strides towards embracing self-love and tenderness lately, too. That impact is being felt right now: self-love and tenderness is sometimes knowing when to walk away.

Turns out the bus station is relatively easy to find, and my bus is leaving in one minute. There's a bus leaving every hour, but I want to leave Leon right away. Every morning has been this way. Keep going, keep moving, new people. On the bus to Astorga, I start to cry. I'm happy and sad all rolled into one, and I am exuding tremendous amounts of emotional steam. I focus on the scenery, which is beautiful, and I discover that I am enjoying myself, despite myself. I can see snow-topped mountains off in the distance. My mind is still muddy when I reach my destination.

Astorga is a stunning assault on my eyes. This place is right out of a damn fairytale. A moat circles the center of town with a cathedral right in the middle of everything. It appears less cathedral and more castle. I certainly have time to take a tour of it now that I'm a bus pilgrim. My next bus doesn't leave for Rabanal for 2 hours. I'm not sure what to do about food. My stomach is still not right. I've been subsisting on digestive cookies and tea. Oh my Lord, I have become a *Cappuccino Pilgrim*!

I found it strange watching pilgrims walk purposefully and steadily over the terrain, while I drifted by on a heated bus. My emotions have been temporarily switched off and I feel nothing at all. I see the young Italian man I helped with his ankle during my time with Marcos. He's taking a bus rest too but will try hiking the 6 km tonight to get to La Cruz. We spend the ride catching up with each other: how we're doing, who we've seen, and of course, our thoughts. He feels like he's cheating the Camino by taking a bus day. "Moi aussi!" I groan. I am the first peregrino to check in to Rabanal because it is only the crack of 11 am. It's an oasis. Marble floors! As if! I sit in the garden and there are small birds flitting all around me. I listen to how loud nature is.

I find the bar and have a tea for my stomach. While I'm there, I see one of the Spanish men from the night outside of Sahagun. Hugs and kisses. *Sigh,* this country suits me. I next meet Co, a man from Holland that I come to really appreciate due to his self- assessment and honesty. I am blown away by his ability to verbalize his emotions and current struggles in life. This self-clairvoyance turns out to be partly due to his training as a psychologist. Duh! He is nonetheless marvellous conversation, and we spend two hours together. He is about 15 years my senior, but the Camino erases these things. While eating lunch, we talk about the strange and wonderful things that have happened to us on the Camino. I urge Co to head back to the albergue with me in order procure him a spot for the night.

I relax on my bed and who shows up but Liz, Spiderman, and… the exhibitionist Portuguese man! Overjoyed isn't the word I'm thinking of. My luck improves when he sets up his ball-slinging cabaret in the bed next to mine. I'm a weirdo magnet. As luck would have it, he decides to take a shower at the same time as me. I get to see the underwear dance all over again, except up close; my own personal private dancer. I didn't even know they sold red thongs after the 1980s. This man is not aware of his personal space. Or worse, maybe he is. No sir, "I don't speak Portuguese."

The word gross isn't strong enough.

Co saves the day and invites me for dinner at 7 pm. I still feel like crap, but I agree to go with him. I haven't eaten much for 4 days, because it's a disaster when I do. I meet a woman at the bar named Anne who knows Co, and we break bread together. She is trying to work via her Ipad on her downtown during the Camino. What downtime? *What downtime?!*

About half way through the meal I have to excuse myself. My body does not want to walk, talk, or eat anymore. If I had an Ipad, its primary function would be as my pillow.

Anne's confidence has made me feel awkward, analyzed, and insecure. I'm one of those people who can't play poker because my face has the words *'Die, fucker'* all over it.

I just know my face is a neon sign right now, but only Co could tell me what it says. I'm immediately reduced by my own undoing into someone who can't communicate intelligently, and I keep saying off-the-wall, idiotic, brainless things. I have the intuition that Co is registering this entire scenario into a diagnosis of some kind, but I don't even mind. I'm exhausted and hallucinating perceived intellectual competition. The fact is Anne is entirely likeable, funny, and competent. The kind of woman I am, usually. Under any normal circumstances she could be my colleague or close friend. I love strong women. I don't know why Anne with her Ipad is bugging me, but it is, and I feel surrender coming on.

I spend the next 8 hours in agony. My stomach is distended and roaring. Anne is probably curled up with her Ipad under a chenille blanket on a portable water bed.

CHAPTER 27

Tranquility

DAY 27 November 08

(Rabanal to El Acebo)

I swear I didn't sleep for more than 5 minutes, but I must have because my eyes have the pleasure of flickering open in time to see the naked Portuguese man's butt crack, standing beside my bed in his red thong. I remind myself to never take a low bunk *ever* again. *When will this madness end?!*

I lay in my bed until he is packed and gone... with my hat pulled down over my whole face. I've been shitting myself stupid all night and I'm in no mood for butt crack.

Co and I go for breakfast, which for me is mint tea. I hike 15 km before I finally collapse. The hike is straight up a mountain; I can see my every breath, it's so cold. There is snow and ice everywhere, but the surrounding mountains are pristine and majestic. It's freezing and extremely windy, but I just want to get off the mountain; I don't care how spectacular it is. Over the past few days, I've found myself losing motivation to finish.

I feel as though I've had my Camino and now I'm punishing myself for no good reason at all. All my yellow arrows are pointing to STOP.

When I reach the famous Cruz de Ferro the weather is atrocious and it would be suicide to stand around for long. I leave my square stone without a meaningful thought in my head. As an afterthought, I take a photo. The day has been unforgiving and yet my sins already so. I reiterate to myself how much I want to be off this mountain. I had hoped for a better frame of mind today but my physical limitations are hindering my spiritual progress.

About 10 km in, the views are getting prettier and prettier. I can see weather moving in fast, and the grey sky is darkening rapidly. I expect that the next 18 km of steady decline into Molinaseca is going to be tough. I want to stop and rest, but to do so would mean freezing into a human popsicle.

By the time I reach El Acebo, I'm wobbling, dizzy and compounded by a glacial numbness. A stop is essential, and I collapse in the closest bar. The hike down to Molinaseca will have to wait until tomorrow. The bar has a fireplace where I want to lie down and sleep... which is kind of what happens anyway. I pass out for 30 minutes, with my head down on the table. Co says I mustn't go on; I simply look awful and I need to stop. I can't disagree. Within 5 minutes, I get myself to a private room overlooking the mountains and sleep for 3 more hours. I can't seem to get warm despite the fireplace. I'm wearing everything in my bag, and I sleep under dry blankets, shivering. If I had more money I'd fly to Bali first thing tomorrow.

I wake, shower with at best tepid water, and head to the bar for my required stamp, where I run into Roberto and Anne. I'm elated to see them both, but especially Roberto whom I've known since day one. He has a raging case of muscle pain, coupled with tendonitis but has managed to walk every step of the trail. My heart swells with pride for his accomplishment. We decide to meet for lunch in Ponferrada tomorrow. He may hike onward. I will try to get there, period. I head back to my little paradise.

The house is spotless, newly renovated, and Himmel, my hospitalero is quiet and gently mannered. He cooks me a delicious vegetarian supper. I want to eat more but with my stomach issues I try only small amounts of what he puts before me. On any other given day, I would have licked the bowls clean; it seems a travesty to waste such beautiful food. It's a dinner for one, but he has laid out a white tablecloth with a tiny vase of flowers enhanced by candlelight. He sends me to my room with a pot of tea and wishes me to feel better. This pampering is just what I needed, and this is the fanciest place I've stayed. I pray tomorrow will be better.

Where are you, inner phoenix?

CHAPTER 28

Co's Kiss

DAY 28 November 09

(El Acebo to Ponferrada 18.5km)

508 km walked.

I wake to the sound of wind blowing. I feel rested from the waist up, but my legs feel like lead. I believe the other name for it is rigor mortis. What the hell are my white blood cells doing anyway? I had a problem with low white blood cell count before and during my cancer treatment, and I'm assuming I still do. I just don't have enough fighter juice in me so it takes me a long time to heal from things. The only time it really bothers me is when I'm this run down. That being said, this is still the best day I've had in good long while, but the truth is, I just don't wanna go anywhere. I descend the candlelit stairway to find Himmel lighting the Buddha. The fire is also lit. The tranquility of this space is akin to a monastery. His life is a peaceful and beautiful one. I feel proud of him for his progress, but in my stupor I forget to tell him that.

Himmel says that it is a warm wind today. "When the wind quits, Heather, know that the rain comes quickly". I appreciate the weather advisory. I may have to splurge on rain pants after all. He brings me tea and toast with goat cheese and his homemade blueberry jam. I'm ravenous, which I take as a good sign. I overpay Himmel for his exceptional care. He responds graciously and with genuine surprise. Good service deserves to be rewarded in my book. I'm not going to make the same mistake I made at the albergue with no beds.

I start to hike and think to myself how I loved this little town with all of its well-kept houses and hospitality. What a magnificent place to collapse!

I pass the place where Co suggested I stay the night. It was goodbye in that instant and he knew it before I did. He asked if he could kiss me goodbye, and thinking he meant on the cheek, I said of course you can. Instead, he found my lips. The kiss was light and incredibly soft and sweet. Everything a simple kiss should be and frankly, I wouldn't have minded another. I was a little caught off guard but had I been more prepared, it may have spoiled it, altogether. What a lovely goodbye for all of our wonderful discussions. *Farewell, my friend.*

I hike about 200 meters and stop for a rest. *Come on, body. Move it.*

The trail to Ponferrada is a slow and rocky descent, slimed with wet rock and mud. The rain showed up on cue as the winds fell away. It's my favourite walk to date, and the air tastes magical. There are wild chestnuts all over the ground. I take a photo of their raw state. I seem to be in a windless microclimate that is humid and jungle like. The towns I pass are empty and quiet, except for feral cats hoping for a crumb or two. A little later, I see Anne and Roberto on the trail. I am extra nice to Anne who's clueless regarding my dilapidated mindset yesterday. It helps that everyone is collectively feeling the physical burn. We stop for fresh eggs and tea to make everything better.

I think of Grizzly who made me fresh eggs the morning I left Canada. I wonder if I'll ever see him again. I've heard that sometimes old lovers become the best of friends. Sounds like torture to me. *Perhaps there is a way to love and not be in love. How do you do that? Does he miss me? Worry?* There's no way to know, and he would never admit to anything. I feel sad for him that he has never let his guard down enough to know true emotional intimacy. *How is that enough?* I'm not sure anymore if I'm missing him in the traditional sense. There's been a shift. I believe it's called "letting go", and what I'm feeling now is a kind of emotional phantom limb; an echo of my heart.

If I'm honest with myself, it wasn't Anne that bugged me yesterday, it was me watching a reflection of myself from the past. Anne and the Camino were reminding me of how overbearing I had become working a stressful and demanding job after realizing my marriage was a sham. It became my shield for pain and dissatisfaction. The betrayal I felt had caused me to become hypervigilant to the things and people surrounding me. I felt on guard, watchful and nervous. I desperately tried to control things that were not in my control by calling it helping. I tried to help people that needed help, when I was the one who needed help. It was the only thing that made me feel better.

The more panicked I felt, the more I tried to tighten the control. The more I controlled the more I was given to control. The control skill came easy to me having learned it from my parents. I'm not sure what their reasons were for controlling behaviour. I have never asked them out of respect for all of the things they did right. It surprised me that I would grow up emulating the qualities I resented being the recipient of. Work piled up and problems at home increased. I never went to sleep feeling as though I had completed everything. I woke up each morning feeling more tired than when I had gone to bed. My emotions were labile and I felt anchored down in misery. I remember looking in the mirror once and wondering how it had come to this. This unhappy woman wasn't me.

I felt ill-equipped for the challenges I faced so I chose the low-hanging fruit of fear and tried to buck up and tolerate my circumstances. Change, or rather the thought of starting all over again, seemed exhausting and completely out of reach; plus, it was scary. I was incapable of fixing or walking away from my life. I believe that all of this aggravation was meant to teach me and then get me so utterly upset that I would naturally leave and create a better reality for myself. I was meant to live a different way; a quiet and peaceful way. I'm a moderate recluse by nature and all of this busy-ness was torture. Of course, the universe knew darn well I wasn't going to get peace and quiet in my environment. I had been given every possible disaster to juggle until I figured that out. The universe kept trying to shout at me to skedaddle, but stubborn people don't listen well at all. I kept juggling all of the balls, and crying in the shower.

My incremental dissatisfaction should have been one of the many markers to lead me onward to better things, but I was committed to the bed I had made for myself. I didn't let up, for years. It was endless and very tiresome. *Don't give up! Keep at it!* and *Practice makes perfect!* were the mantras of my youth. Delegating a task would have been unthinkable back then; absolute weakness. I feared that if I didn't keep things perfect, I would fall apart; but falling apart was exactly what I needed.

Perfection is the hardest act to keep up. I felt like a gerbil running on its wheel; running and running with no end in sight. No profit or distance gained. When I think back to my childhood pet gerbil, he finally ate his red wheel in its entirety; broke out of his cage, then out of my room into a big wide world of freedom. I wanted to be a gerbil. I wanted more than anything to be so small no one would notice that I had vanished.

But how could I have left? Quitting my well-paying job would have been an act of madness. That would have been impractical and foolish. To leave a marriage I just entered into would be giving up too easily. I was the queen of justifying my mess of a life. My girlfriend asked me every year, "When are you going to leave him?" I would reply, "Not yet, I'm not ready. Give me another year." I resisted the notion that if I walked away from everything, it would mean failure. I would have had to have been accountable for my half of the equation and I wasn't ready to face that. My heart was in a good place and applying effort was my way of showing it; no matter how misguided or ineffective it had turned out to be.

Sometimes it is good to throw in the towel. The trick in life is knowing *when* to let go and for which things.

Researching different religions in later years taught me about the problems people have with attachment. Apparently, it binds the soul to earthly things and people, which keeps us in a constant pattern of rebirth. If you don't want to come back to earth anymore, for yet another helping of life's drama, then stop wanting things. The books make it sound easy.

Anyway, by then I had become a collector of people and things. I didn't know you didn't need to keep everyone. When my relationships got toxic, I kept them around for several more years before annihilating them, when I could have politely let them drift. I hadn't the emotional maturity to know there are a thousand ways to skin a cat. Meditation has thankfully helped me with this kind of people-hoarding behaviour. The pause and the breath is usually all the time you need to redirect to a higher place when dealing with anyone or anything.

I have to remind myself today *that* was the old Heather, because it almost sounds like hearing about somebody else. When that time of year came around again, and my friend asked me, "When are you going to leave him", my answer was still the same. Except I had made one adjustment: I switched my email password to *Freedom365*. The daily reminder of logging on must have planted tiny seeds of hope and possibility. I was home to Canada within 9 months of that one tiny change.

I clearly recall how everything finally collapsed and how everything I had worked so hard for was now gone. It was a truly awful period of my life, but on the flipside, I noticed peace and quiet starting to permeate into my every day.

Once I got back to Canada, I spent a lot of time creating a dream board with motivating pictures and words; things I strongly believed would bring me balance, and it was a symbolic collage of what I needed my life to become. I stared at the darn thing every single day. A few years later, I realized that everything on the board had come true, except my goal to learn Spanish, which is hilarious because here I am in yet another Spanish country wishing I could speak Spanish. I guess learning the language wasn't essential to my soul. I didn't *need* it, I just *wanted* it. Huh!

Peace felt medicinal, and there was no dollar value for that. My shoulders soon came down from up around my ears and my laughter didn't sound as strained. Eventually, I picked up the pieces of my life while meditating close to 20 hours a week; before work, after work, on my breaks, and so forth. My soul was aching for healing and I kneeled to it willingly. It was the first of many sacrifices that I would make for my soul.

I feared that if I didn't grow and change, I would create the very same life I had fled. If I wanted happy, peaceful people in my life, then I needed to become a happy, peaceful person. Whatever it was that I wanted in this life, I needed to be able to reflect back from inside myself. I had never listened to what my heart was telling me, and it turns out it had quite a bit to say. Now more than anything I wanted a PhD in *me*, and that's where I was going to invest my time. Everything else in life was proving to be tangible, anyway. What I needed was solid ground and my feet squarely on it. Soul work was a decent place to start. I felt like springtime and knew I was growing; it was about time. I was 34 years old.

As I poured my time into meditation, I also poured love into my patients as a nurse. I saved my money and stared at my dream board. I knew that if I stayed true to my heart, my life would become something beyond my wildest dreams. And it did. Whatever I had lost, I gained back in knowledge and wisdom by having lived a wild story. I was never one to learn vicariously through someone else's experiences. I was good listener, but couldn't apply the lessons to my own life. I was one of those people who had to come around the corner skidding on her chin; I had to go through it to learn it.

So Anne, I have to thank you from the bottom of my heart for your wisdom and urgent reflection on my life. I do not think ill of you or any of my teachers along The Way. They have been brutally honest with me. I didn't love it, but I drank it down. I'm walking and reflecting and learning how to be better, and I have to say, it was a whole lot easier when I was only worrying about blisters.

I hike the last 8 km with Roberto. We stop at the first café and have an espresso with cognac: our traditional friendship drink. It's strong and good. Roberto tells me that yesterday was a huge day for him at La Cruz de Ferro. His tells me that his brother had become addicted to drugs a few years back and had admitted to him that he was drug running in 2008. The last time Roberto spoke to him was July of that year, and his brother has been missing ever since. His family has been devastated by this and suffered much depression in the aftermath. They've tried counselling both together and separately, but have essentially stopped living. Their lives have been on pause because authorities have not been able to provide any evidence in the case. Roberto has set up a webpage to try to find his brother, has utilized Facebook, and has spoken with the missing persons department in Italy. He has tried desperately to bring closure for his parents and himself.

Yesterday, he accepted the fact that he has to walk the Camino for himself and not his brother. If his brother wants to contact him, then it is up to him to do so. He has accepted his brother's lifestyle as a homeless wanderer. Roberto has to let his brother go and be who he has to be. He admits that he has been looking every single day on the trail for the face of his brother and that he feels close to him. He admits his brother is probably dead, but regardless, he has to stop being depressed. Roberto says he wants his life back. "I'm alive, I should live". I tell him that this is *huge* progress. He has truly had his Camino now. My enlightenment was in Los Arcos and his at the Cruz de Ferro. We cheers to each other.

Anything else that happens for us on the Camino will be additional bounty. We agree to celebrate in style tonight for our personal pilgrimages; for our very lives.

Ponferrada is famous for its *mesons*, The Knights Templar, and there is a castle honouring this history. The castle is a 12th century building called the Castillo de los Templarios. There is only one open refugio on the edge of town and it looks pretty dodgy. We strut past it, straight into the main square with our packs. We get a hotel and pay out our asses for the most outstanding view of the castle. We stand on our balcony and watch the sun set. This is the life.

The hotel walls are made of stone, giving it castle decorum. There are two single beds, a personal balcony, and our very own bathroom. We send our laundry out for someone else to do, like we're royalty. I DO feel like a princess. Maybe Tonni was right afterall.

Like children, Roberto and I race across the street and check out the castle. There is an amazing romantic and masculine energy to the grounds. I can picture the occupants of the past. It's exhilarating. I'm not much of a history buff, but this place is as mysterious as it is intriguing. I plan to research it more if I ever make it home again. There are documents and books sealed by the Vatican at the castle library. The writing and colourful pages are more beautiful than any artwork I've ever seen. There are spiral staircases, cannons, and holes in the walls where cannons were placed during the war. I smell battle.

I imagine horses, vintage clothing, armour, and swords. *Have I been here before?* It feels oddly familiar. I picture what women must have looked like back then. What I would have looked like back then. Would I have possessed a quiet female strength while appearing entirely delicate? Doubt it. I apply these attributes to my vision because they are qualities I wish I had.

The day is grey and dreary, which makes for excellent castle photography. After our tour, we immediately go to a bar like good knights do, and drink gigantic beers. We talk for an hour or so and decide to go shopping, where I finally breakdown and buy waterproof pants and a new t-shirt. The t-shirt is an added luxury, but I've lost so much weight on this trip that my saggy clothes look like they belong to someone else. I fit into XS pants now. If I weighed myself, I think I would be frightened. Only bones and muscle remain, giving me the lean look of runway gauntness. My breasts and ass have simply vanished.

Next, we hit the pharmacy, where Roberto gets new insert soles for his boots. He throws in tendonitis ointment as an afterthought. The supermercado is our candyland where we spare no expense. We buy a 2008 Rioja red wine, caviar, crackers, jamon and queso. We eat our treasures on the balcony and talk for hours in a peaceful epitome of hanging out. It's one of those nights where you want to freeze time. It could have only been improved by being here with someone that I wanted to make love to, but since I can't have that, being with a terrific friend is the very next best thing.

Roberto spends hours trimming his soles to perfection. This is my first time ever eating caviar so I pay no attention to him and lose myself in all the flavours before me. What could be better than this view? Buskers are playing their guitars and flutes below us on the street and are unaware of our presence. What a great night!

We eat supper at an Italian restaurant in honour of Roberto. We order a bottle of Chianti and plates of pasta. We are a tipsy happy. Roberto tells me about Italy and I tell him about Canada. Such different lives we live. We decide we should go to Oktoberfest next year and visit Thomas who lives in Germany. We tuck ourselves into clean sheets in our warm beds, and sleep blissfully like children.

CHAPTER 29

Survivor Guilt

DAY 29 Friday, November 10

(Ponferrada to Sarria)

Little bit headache. How much wine did we have? At 8:00 am we head downstairs and have a coffee together. Roberto is walking on, and I'm taking a train to Sarria, 94.3 km away. I have already chopped off 66.8 km already. The trail from Sarria to Santiago is roughly 100 km; all a pilgrim is required to do to get a Compostela. You must do it either by walking those 100 km or by biking 200 km on the last part of the trail, consecutively. I know my body is going to whine but I will take my time and try to enjoy the walk. 18 km is plenty before I'm ready to call it quits for the day. I will have time to go to Finisterre, I think. The thought lifts me. I have some leeway now, unless something else crops up.

Roberto and I say goodbye. He goes one way and I go another. As usual, I'm tearful. I'm awful with goodbyes. If I don't see him in Santiago, I will hopefully see him in Munich next year. I can live with that. I arrive at the train station by 8:30 am, after some trial and error. I don't have a schedule, but I'm hoping something leaves within the hour. For €15, I can relax and ride the 3 hours to Sarria. Even though my Camino is already completed, other pilgrims will be just starting theirs. I stare in disbelief at the ticket because the train leaves at 4 pm which will mean a 7.5 hour wait. The ticket-booth lady then informs me that it's never on time.

I take the time to catch up on my journaling at the station. I drink the worst coffee of my life and watch some lady's dog take a shit right in the middle of the bar. You've got to love Spain. I'm a bit worried about my feet. Everything skinwise has healed but I've had some nerve damage since Puenta la Reina. From the balls of my feet to the tip of each great toe is numb. *Is this going to be for life?*

I'm still having irregular (premature ventricular) heartbeats that sometimes give over to short runs. I know this because I can feel them in my chest and when I check my wrist pulse. Something is not right. It happens more frequently when I'm dehydrated, so I'd better fill up. I can understand all of the crosses along the way now, and I know I've pushed my body to the brink. I've been cavalier.

I miss my dog, my bed, and my life back home. I appreciated them before, but there's nothing like time away to make the heart grow fonder. I re-affirm that I'm not afraid to die. And I'm not. There were a few nights after chemotherapy treatment when I thought for sure I wouldn't wake. I wasn't scared, just bone tired. I had made peace with death and had given over to the idea that it might very well be my time. What I feared most was physical pain, and I was having difficulty enduring the suffering. Death to me had become nothing more than a release I frankly wouldn't have minded. Life was really, really hard back then. If I had died, I wouldn't have had to solve any of my problems.

I still feel an overwhelming amount of survivor guilt for living when other friends of mine have died. Friends that had husbands and children that needed them. I don't have any of that. My death would therefore have been less impactful? Did I really believe my life wasn't worth as much as theirs? I can't say. All I know for sure is that I have Survivor Guilt and it plagues me.

I'm not afraid to die, but on the flip side, I've been too busy being afraid to live. I pick men to date that I know I will never have longevity with. It might be me that has the intimacy and commitment issues. And rightly so, I justify. If I'm going to live, then I should get busy and grab more from life. I have things to do. I think about my responsibilities, if any, regarding the things I've seen and learned along The Way. *What now? What's next?*

Well for starters, I'm starving.

I figure that if the food at the train station is as delightful as the coffee and the atmosphere, I should just pass. I grab my backpack and go in search of nibbles. This is a small problem in Spain. It's coffee and bread for breakfast, and nothing for lunch until bocadillos become available around 4pm, with supper much later on. I'm desperate.

The first restaurant I walk into, a bartender stares at me unbelievingly. He looks surprised and confused to see a customer. He tells me that there is no food until night time. Of course, but it was worth a try. *Does anybody eat in the middle of the day in this country? Could this be why the locals are adorably short and slim? Are they stunted by starvation?* I keep walking. THERE HAS TO BE FOOD SOMEWHERE! By some miracle, after walking around for miles I find a deli, or rather Ali Babba's Cave. I feel giddy, my fingertips gathered at my lips. I buy a family pack of chickpea stew, penne with chicken in a red sauce, one large roasted pimento, 2 pastries, and canned beer.

I leave with my prizes and head for a beautiful park of trees covered in morning fog; a picnic just for one. Pleased with my resourcefulness and my own company, I eat everything. Every single bite. It's a bit early for beer but if my heart is going to flutter and stop, I'd rather do it on a full stomach with a bit of a buzz.

Oh geez, four more hours until my train boards. I should be sightseeing, I suppose, but I take the time to stretch out and relax in the sunlight. I think I will read the guidebook Tonni has left for me. It's really a treat, because today is the first time I've seen a map. I have walked this whole thing by instinct and faith. I am ready to take in some factoids seeing as I have the time.

THE PILGRIM'S STONE

Risk

To laugh is to risk appearing a fool,
To weep is to risk being called sentimental,
To reach out to another is to risk involvement,
To expose feeling is to risk exposing your true self,
To place your ideas and dreams before a crowd is to risk their loss,
To love is to risk not being loved in return,
To live is to risk failure.
But risks must be taken because the
greatest hazard in life is to risk nothing.
The person who risks nothing does nothing,
has nothing, is nothing.
He may avoid suffering and sorrow,
But they cannot learn, feel, change, grow or live.
Chained by his servitude, he is a slave
who have forfeited all freedom.
Only a person who risks is free.

—William Arthur Ward

That poem is the only thing I really needed to read off any map or guidebook. I think I am free. I think if I am dependent on the behaviour or actions of others for my sense of serenity, I will never stay free. What excellent advice; thank you, Mr. William Ward.

The train to Sarria is 40 minutes late, and I'm under the impression "it comes when it comes". The ticket says Gate 3, so I walk down the tunnel and am redirected by an old woman who tells me in Spanish it's actually Gate 2. On board the train, I daydream and sleep on and off, all the way to my destination. It's a beautiful lush, mountainous terrain. I'm relieved

SURVIVOR GUILT

to be sitting even though I've been sitting all day. My desire to walk is non-existent.

When I depart from the train, there are no signs. I get in stride with another pilgrim who seems to know the way. His name is Joshua, and he's from Winnipeg. He's 18 years old and returning from Santiago. He has taken a year off school to build his confidence and figure out what he wants to do with his life. I think it is wonderful he has this opportunity and think more young people should take a gap year.

He tells me he has learned everything the hard way and left garbage bags of his things hidden behind old churches along The Way. I'm not sure if he means he's learned things the hard way on the Camino or in life in general. I don't ask him to clarify because he's venting. He tells me that he has to head back at some point to get his hidden garbage bags of stuff. I hope for his sake these things are still around for him. I mutter to Joshua, "Oh, now don't feel too bad about things. I think I've been doing things the hard way for a quite a while now too." I'm thinking about the garbage bags and their similarity to emotional baggage. I would love to leave some of mine behind a church somewhere and not go back for it… ever.

We find an albergue and check in. It's clean and nice, but the shower water is glacial. The lights turn off every minute or two, so I'm showering in ice cold water… in the dark. I wonder if bad people have to do this kind of thing in Hell for all eternity.

The Spanish fellow from Basque whom I met in Bercianos with Tonni is at our albergue tonight. I say "Hey Basque, how goes the struggle?" even though I know he speaks no English. He recognizes me and I get an enthusiastic, albeit sweaty greeting in return. I see the Israeli couple from earlier in the trail also. It's a warm feeling to see familiar faces after zipping ahead about 160 km.

Joshua and I find a supermercado and get oranges, bananas, apple tort, bread, cheese, and jamon for breakfast. We seem to buy the heaviest things that a store can sell to people who have to carry them. The refugio serves supper for €10 and on location. The decision to stay is an easy one. It's an average meal but the wine is decent. I'm a foodie, so I'm starting to find the dinners repetitive. Pilgrims need a lot of calories, so in the end you might as well get something in you; anything at all.

I sleep like angels must and wake up at 7:30 am. It's staying dark later and later, so it's hard to tell when to wake up; I have no alarm clock either.

THE PILGRIM'S STONE

I share my breakfast 3 ways with my bunkmates. Joshua is staying here for a few days to relax, since he has the time. He has a whole year to Camino. I'm not sure if that would be a blessing or a curse. Basque says he will hike 40 km today, while I imagine I will be fortunate enough to master 20 km. Fast or slow, it doesn't matter; the Camino will catch up to you. It happens to be really smart that way.

CHAPTER 30

Gerhild

DAY 30 Saturday November 11
(Sarria to Portomarin 20km)

I feel a renewed excitement and energy to walk the Camino again. It's the last stretch to Santiago and I actually feel joy and happiness permeating my heart. I had forgotten briefly what joy and happiness felt like. Today happens to be my friends' wedding back home. I'm thinking of them and wishing that their day is beautiful and perfect. I'm thinking of my home, my life, and the people in it. I know I should be contacting people back home but I've enjoyed being off the grid. I did try once, but I'd forgotten my Hotmail password and couldn't figure out how to change it using Spanish prompts. That's how often I use the internet. Yes, the computers are Spanish in Spain. All of my friends gave me their addresses and email accounts. The few that gave addresses have already been sent postcards. I like travelling without the pressure to stay connected. Sure, the world has become fast and efficient, but are we really making meaningful connections anymore?

The first 2 hours of my walk is cluttered with noisy, chattering people. It's a real contrast from the earlier parts of the trail. It is pouring rain, but alas, I have waterproofed myself in my new Gore-Tex pants. It's not too cold outside either; that, or my fever has broken. I'm not used to so many pilgrims being on the trail and it irritates me that I can't be alone in nature. I want to think my thoughts in peace, but all I hear are happy pilgrims on the first day of their Camino. *Try to be nice now, Heather.*

Many people come to Spain, do this last 100 km stretch of the St. James Way, and get their Compostela in this fashion. Not everyone has the desire or luxury of time to do the whole thing in one shot. Other pilgrims do The Way in stages over several years. All ways are the best ways and any Camino is better than no Camino, in my book. I'm beginning to understand the magic of this trail. I imagine that if a pilgrim only walked 100 km, they could still very well get the soul shake they are looking for. For the willing and those who are ready to listen.

All the happy, noisy pilgrims stop in the first bar. I take a quick coffee and keep on hiking. I want to stay ahead of them. Luck is with me and I get my alone time for the remainder of the day. This is my kind of heaven. The landscape is lush and gorgeous, with mountains everywhere. I feel youthful and happy, and I feel the universe by my side. I am lighter than I've ever felt before. I have no physical pain, my stomach is good, my feet are excellent, and I feel rested. Every step is effortless. I stop on a craggy rock fence to reflect and pray. For the time that I sit, the rain stops and the sun blazes for the duration of my prayer. I shut my eyes and lift my face to the sky. It feels like i'm getting a wink from God; it's a sublime moment. The minute I put my backpack on, the rain begins again, as though it had stopped just for me to rest.

Today the trail snakes between apple groves, chestnut trees, wild blackberries, and scrub heather. I had never seen wild heather growing anywhere, before. Docile lambs and horses, smelly pigs and cows dot the countryside. The small villages are as beautiful as they are poor. I remind myself that I would have missed all of this if I had packed up and gone home.

I spend a great deal of time thinking about my little brother, Josh. I met Josh when he was 9 years old, through the Big Brothers, Big Sisters program, and he has filled a gap in my life, never having had any children of my own. I think Josh would really love doing a Camino. He's had far too many struggles in his young life. I pick up a stone and ask God that his sorrows be released from him and absorbed into this little rock.

I cross a long bridge that brings me into Portomarin. The river below is wide and dark. I pause to take it in. My desire today was to hike alone in nature, and my wish was granted for me. I feel mentally refreshed and it has been a marvellous day all the way down to my numbed toes. I stop at a bar that serves only pizza and spaghetti. Things are really looking up for me these days. Anything to get out of the rain is a dream come true, but adding pasta doesn't hurt. I talk with the owner in a mix of Spanish and French; my usual mumbo jumbo that nobody understands. I really need to sign up for Spanish lessons when I get home . He starts a fire in the wood stove and makes a gigantic spaghetti Bolognese for me. I drink half a bottle of his best wine by 2:30 pm. He tells me that he's done the Camino four times so far. He's originally from Tuscany, Italy, but explains that there is no work there. I'm puzzled by this because everyone in Spain has told me there's no work in Spain.

A woman about my age walks in out of the rain. There's only one table in the bar, so I acquiesce, and we eat together. I'm done hiking, therefore, my sociability is re-emerging. The woman's name is Gerhild, and we hit it off straight away. I tell her of my plans to go to Germany for Oktoberfest in the fall and that I'll give her a call when I get there. We exchange numbers and take photos before parting. She says she will be hiking on today and I wish her a buen Camino.

What I'm learning from this Camino is that I have no substantial problems; issues yes, but no substantial problems. Everyone I meet is unemployed, homeless, grieving, or looking for someone or something. I miss my dog. Now that my feet don't hurt, I haven't anything at all to complain about. I'm sure anybody reading this is relieved to hear it.

I check into a clean, empty albergue recommended by the restaurant owner. I can pick whatever bed I want. I have a window and a heater next to my bed. I couldn't have wished my circumstances to be better. I can pretty much bet there will be hot water because I'm the first one here. Did you hear that? First. Not last. First. Not that I'm kicking any Camino ass or anything, but I'm feeling pretty proud of myself. I don't dare jinx myself with further accolades and draw upon myself a host of locust and boils.

I shower with bona fide hot water, the lights are *on*, and I mow my legs. I'm in the Holiday Inn, as far as I'm concerned. I have oodles of products left and I have subsisted off of 5 ounces each of shampoo and conditioner for my hair, face cleanser, and deodorant for five weeks now. No doubt I'm probably not getting the same clean but it still shocks me when I think about how much I waste in Canada. I thought I was living a simple life, but in all honesty, I've still been living in too much lux. I wonder if I will incorporate some additional frugalness into my life when I return.

Alas, I hit the supermercado and make a decision to cook tonight at the albergue. I get garbanzo beans, green chillies, onion and wine, with a side of breakfast food. I mess up royally up by walking past the cosmetics aisle and buying not one, but *two* perfume spritzes. One is floral scented and the other a musk to appease my split personality, I guess.

And that's how frugality went out the window.

I can't help myself. I have reeked for weeks on end justifying this 60 mL of liquid foolishness, because I'm the idiot that has to carry it anyway. I'm running out of room in my journal so I pick up another one and a couple of pens. Who knew I had so much to say?

CHAPTER 31

No Cochina!

DAY 31 November 12

(Portomarin to Palas de Rei to Casanova, a small town that is closed 32 km +/- Taxi to Melide.)

Nobody is awake at 8:30 am in the albergue as I walk out the door. I'm dressed for rain even though it's sunny at the moment. I know how this country works.

I see my German friend Gerhild up ahead. She didn't walk on yesterday as she had planned. As soon as she had walked past the albergue, she felt pulled inside by an invisible hand. We hike together off and on all day. She is not overly chatty, but she's sweet as berry pie. She's my kind of gal. We are both a bit tired, so we take it slow. Or in other words: slow pilgrims taking it slower.

We only get lost three times, but who's counting? We stop in every bar for a warm-up coffee, bocadillo, and/or beer, as we go merrily along in the rain. It does, however, stop raining for about five minutes at one point, and the sky unfolds for us a lovely rainbow. That's new. It's proof of no rain.

There's a noisy bunch of young pilgrims, and I shrink inwardly. I'm in a different space these days and the gap has become too wide for me to bridge. We decide to hike on past them another 8 km and hope that they stay in the previous town for the night. I'm already bushed but my friend urges me on. All is well until we get to Casanova and learn that the albergue has no restaurant. There is no bar or food in the town at all. "NO KITCHEN!" shouts an angry hospitalero in broken English. This woman seems extremely annoyed by our presence. She shouts again, "NO COCHINA!" She is right incensed, spewing indignance, while Gerhild and I stare at her placid as cows. It's really the first time I've ever been chased out of town. Over my shoulder I say "*That's alright, Mum, I only have garlic and a tangerine.*" She begrudgingly gives us information regarding another albergue, with a restaurant and a hotel, 2 km ahead while waving us away with her arms.

We have about an hour of daylight left so we'd better get moving. We stumble onward, and almost panic when we don't see a town 2 km ahead. We find it bit farther, which in the end doesn't really matter because the entire town is closed from front to back. Ohhhh! That naughty lying *witch*!

Some swearing ensues until we conference and decide to phone a taxi for a ride to anywhere. Being the honest pilgrims we are and for our conscience, we'll taxi back tomorrow.

At this time of year, albergues aren't necessarily open, and restaurants are hit and miss. One thing Heather cannot miss is dinner, so it's *bon appetit* in Melide. I eat two entrees and drink half a bottle of wine.

I have become a bloody Viking.

CHAPTER 32

Grocery Store Perfume

DAY 32 November 13

(Melide back to O Coto to Melide to Arzua)

For €5, the albergue has only cold water, so no shower for me. I just can't bear it, so I go to bed filthy after a 32 km hike, sleep in my hiking clothes, and hike in them again the next day. I've reached a new standard of rock bottom. I've lost the will to clean my body. But nobody worry, I have grocery store perfume that I spray generously over both Gerhild and myself.

We do the right thing. We take a taxi from Melide to O Coto and pick up where we left off yesterday. We meet up with two Canadians from Toronto, Gord and Monica, who are both artists by trade. We hike *muy rapido* back to Melide. Which is way too *rapido* for me, and I take a little break while they dash off at breakneck speed. I groan, classifying them as not-even-human.

Gerhild and I are about the same pace, so we go all the way to Arzua together, taking in a little local cuisine along the way. Did you know that Arzua is best known for its cheese? Gerhild urges me to try a beer with lemon juice in it. I'm not an immediate fan but the change is nice. Germans apparently put anything in their beers. I notice that I'm leaning forward to hear more about it. I'm finding it harder and harder to hike tipsy. It is, to my recollection, the first full, sunny day, and without a hint of wind, which is outstanding because I was beginning to think Spain didn't have a sun.

I decide not to push my luck, so I take a spot at a private albergue. Gerhild wants to hike 18 km more today; I tell her she's nutso. It is already 3:30 pm, and the way the albergues are lately, I wouldn't want to be stuck without food or a place to sleep. There is literally nothing for her until St. Irene, so I hope for her sake there is a bed for her tonight.

The albergue is perfect: it's new and it has hot water. It has a garden area to sit in and a large kitchen where I meet a colourful character from Brazil named Flavio. He is overjoyed that I have agreed to cook for us tonight. I plan for a feast and gather enough supplies for any additional guests that may be at our table. Chris (Africa) and Ildhie (Hungary) join us for pasta, salad, and fresh bread. We eat so much that our bellies are bursting.

It's an international group and unfortunately I am only fluent in English. Flavio speaks Portuguese, Spanish, and some English, Chris has his Afrikaans and English, Ildhie mostly uses her smiling and hand gestures because she doesn't speak any of these languages and none of us speak Hungarian. Food and drink are universal, and from the sounds and sighs, I gather we are all satisfied with the food. We are the only 4 people in the building and it's a perfect party. The dishes are done for me, which leaves me time to sit outside. I stare up at the big clear sky filled with twinkling stars, and breathe thanks. Later on, I spritz some grocery store perfume under my armpits and drift blissfully off to sleep.

CHAPTER 33

Flavio "The Great"

DAY 33 November 14

(Arzua to Arca do Pino 20.5 km)

Oh, Shitballs! It's 8:00 am and the room is dark. We've all slept in. I pack up quickly and eat the tangerines and yogurt Flavio and I bought yesterday. All this rushing is really a facade because I know I won't hike a step, if it can be helped, without café con leche. Usually there is a bar 50 meters in any direction from the albergues, and today is no different, except they're all brimming with pilgrims.

I hike the day with my cheerful companion, Flavio, who is starved for human contact. He has just hiked the Camino North, which is by the sea and counted 12 pilgrims, other than himself. He tells me it's mountainous, but the ocean views made up for it. I look at every single one of his two thousand photographs and picture myself in those places.

Flavio smiles all the time and doesn't talk much while he is hiking. I can't say I mirror the smiling portion, but I also don't talk that much while I walk. It's really enough of an effort to hike and beat my fucking heart. I am not at liberty to fritter away energy making words come out. Communication is mostly futile anyway because his languages are Portuguese and Spanish with a dab of English. When he does speak, it is in Portuguese, so it might as well be Japanese or Klingon. I wonder what on earth he is saying. He's as pleasant as the sun, itself. I'll give him that.

The trail winds itself through forested areas mixed with farmland full of cows, sheep, and cornfields. A mist covers the valley we've just walked through, even though the sun is shining brightly. Flavio sings beautiful songs in Portuguese off and on during the hike. His voice is easy to listen to and find I am smiling along with him. He asks me to sing for him. I tell him I cannot because I have no guitar. I don't know why I won't sing for him. I guess I've always felt shy without an instrument to hide behind. He doesn't have a guitar with him, but he does have his Brazilian flag strapped to the outside of his backpack. Alas, I mentally dub him as Flavio the Great. He's so proud of that flag that I just don't have the heart to tell him he looks like a tiny superhero.

We stop for a lunch of leftover food from last night, while we soak up the sun. We drink a cold beer in our little sunny paradise and watch cows march themselves down the main street. It's been two days since we've had any wind or rain. Even the rain man needs a day off now and again. I give him a thumbs up.

We stop at another bar about 5 km up the road for another couple of beers to go with our meats and cheese. There will be no awards today given out for speed. We sit and talk with two guys from Spain... in Spanish. My eyes are glazing over. I feel like Ildhie from Hungary, who was smiling and hand gesturing all evening; which is exactly what I'm doing now. I remember thinking how deranged Ildhie seemed due to the language barrier and now I'm living that dream myself.

Back on the trail, I see Veronica from Catalonia who had had problems with her back in Burgos. We embrace. She looks emotionally light as a feather and I'm so glad to see she's having a happy ending to her Camino. She tells me to stop by sometime at her bar in the south of Spain. It's on the beach! We exchange contact information just in case. We hope to meet up in Santiago for some dancing, eating, and celebrating. I'm getting really excited to reach Santiago. I hope it lives up to its reputation, because it's been an awfully long walk to get there.

Later, I meet Vicki, a woman from Texas who just cracks me up. She's the definition of funny. Oh, how I love funny people! If there was only an ethical way to genetically engineer the human race for the purpose of creating funnier people. How could there be war at all, if everyone was bowled over in laughter? Literally, every facial expression and word spoken by this woman erupted gales of laughter from anyone within earshot. My sides are in stitches, and by the time we call it a night I feel as though I've executed 40,000 crunches.

She later tells me a story about how her own life is kind of on hold while she takes care of her mother. I contemplate how selfless and loving that is, but it comes out in jest as,

"Well, you're doing a CRAPPY job of caring for her at the *moment*."

I've lost my goddam filter. With widened eyes, my hand drifts upward in an effort to cover my mouth. Thankfully, she doubles over in laughter. Vicki understands all too well how to handle stress with humour. It's an outstanding coping mechanism. I guess it's true that when life gives you tough things to handle, laughter is still the best medicine.

I end up getting a hostel with Flavio, which is probably a mistake in hindsight, but I want hot water and a firm bed without a sea of pilgrim eyes watching my every move. I can handle one set of eyes. This is the second time on this trip that I'm staying in a hotel with a man platonically, but I feel as though I really have to make my intentions clear this time. Flavio the Great is looking entirely too hopeful. In an effort to economize my speech, I blurt out, "Separate beds, hombre!" Can't really blame a feller for trying, I suppose. I guess I should feel flattered being a single middle-aged woman, but sex is just not on my agenda; not while I'm walking on the trail and working on my soul.

The shower is worth the fuss. I tell Flavio that I plan to splurge on a room all to myself in Santiago. I had only meant to express my dream out loud as conversation, but the poor chap looked hurt. Oh, poor, sweet Flavio, you will find your lady love one day, I'm sure of it. Wait a minute, I've been thinking short-term. It doesn't end in Santiago with securing a solo hotel room. I remind myself that I have a HOUSE to go back to in Canada. Oh my God, that's *right*!

"Vive la Camino, and vive la… real life!"

I go to bed thinking about this elusive place called Finisterre. I hope it's possible to take a bus up there so I can see what the end of the world is like. These pills are burning a hole in my pocket.

CHAPTER 34

Victory Lap

DAY 34 November 15

(Arca do Pino to Santiago 21 km)

This is it! My last day of Tamoxifen pills; my cancer treatment is officially done, as of right now. Woot! Woot! I'm glad I planned my trip around this monumental day. I love what this drug has done for me, but not at all how it made me feel. The shackles are off, and I've earned my freedom.

But for how long? Am I really cured? Or will it start coming back once I stop taking this drug. I tuck away these thoughts, but I'm a bit nervous to stop taking them. They've been my crutch; my safety net. I won't have to see the bottle on the sink every morning. I won't have the daily reminder that I went through something terrible. Frankly, I don't ever want to see the pills ever again. I wouldn't be able to bear it a second time around.

Today I will march my skinny ass and legs 21 km into Santiago. It takes me and Flavio a bit to find the trail, again, mostly because of me. I don't tell him about the pills. I can't. I'm trying to figure out how I'm feeling about it all. I'm worried that I will break the spell; like waking from a beautiful dream and then realizing the dream isn't real life.

I find mornings in general are a bit rough, and I spin-cycled us in the wrong direction a teensy bit. Flavio, being Flavio, is just happy to be walking anywhere with anybody. I take full accountability for my confidently bold lack of direction, and apologize to Flavio.

Think about it, Heather.

Have you ever, even once, before this Camino, EVER, even ONE TIME, EVER jumped out of bed and gone hiking for six hours?

Exactly!

The towns we pass seem more affluent and are at least better maintained as we walk towards Santiago. I let my mind travel where it wants, but what I want is to hike into Santiago alone. I need to shake off Flavio, but I don't how to do it. My thoughts are rude, and it doesn't occur to me at the time to simply ask him if he would mind. Why do I feel like I need anyone's permission? I devise a plan to hike ahead and "lose" him naturally, somehow. The last thing I want to do is hike into Santiago with a man. I just want to walk into Santiago with just Heather; no clapping, no fuss, no kiss, hug, no weirdo anything. Just to arrive.

Well, maybe clapping wouldn't be terrible.

At the moment of commitment,
The entire universe
Conspires to assist you."
–GOETHE

Flavio and I stop for lunch about 10 km outside of Santiago. We join two Bulgarian fellows who are cycling the North Camino. We cheers our beers. Flavio orders something for me as if he knows what I want to eat. I realize he is just being polite and chivalrous but "Por favor," I say, "I would like to order for myself, if that's okay." He seems genuinely surprised. I want to wrinkle my nose and evaporate into thin air. *Poof.* I don't know why I'm getting so uptight.

I dodge Flavio unceremoniously about 5 km out of Santiago. I duck into a bar after hiking ahead to stop for a coke. When I get back from the bathroom, the bartender has put a large bowl of lentil stew in front of me. It's mouth-wateringly good. I didn't even know I was hungry. I nod in thanks to the sweet bartender, but he's looking at me like I'm a species he's never seen before.

I think about Flavio and hope I haven't hurt his feelings too badly. I really am a mess at setting boundaries. Why couldn't I have just said "Hey, Flavio I need to do this alone"? Simple right? Nope. Not for me. Perhaps my experience with Marcos has made me think I wouldn't be able to get away if I had tried that strategy. Walking into Santiago is too important for me to risk having anyone beside me. I need to do this alone on my own steam, and I sacrificed poor Flavio to do it.

The path of the pilgrim has a few perks, but I have been getting nods of respect from the locals and nods of understanding from other pilgrims. I wonder if finally getting to Santiago will be anticlimactic. Magical? Mysterious? Awesome? I plan to spend some major cash on a nice room tonight. Solo. Just me, myself, and I. On my own! My, my, now look who can be clear about things when she wants to be!

Lo and behold, I see Santiago. It's big and it's BEAUTIFUL! I love it already! Truly. It looks sparkling clean and bustling from way up here on the hill. And as I walk down into the valley, cross the bridge, and enter the park, there is actually clapping and cheering. *For me?!* It's a group of fellow pilgrims from days past. They've been in the park cheering the pilgrims coming into Santiago for the past three hours. They've rolled out their bed mats, turned on some music, and are sharing their chocolate and wine with me. They are drinking the wine from a filthy pilgrim cup. This is my kind of impromptu party. They are set up in a median between rush hour traffic, on a small patch of lush green grass.

It's all fairly conspicuous.

Some of the locals wave to us, and the rest are trying very hard to avoid eye contact. We do look like a ragged bunch. I'm not sure, if I saw the looks of ME anywhere but here, that I'd make eye contact either.

We made it! We are in Santiago!!

Suddenly my backpack feels like air. How is that possible? I know that I've gotten stronger with all of the hiking, but it literally feels weightless. Everything I needed was on my back for over a month; my cross to bear, my sins. Many, many people have told me they thought my pack was too heavy to carry. I think my pack was just right... for me. I needed to carry exactly the amount of weight that I did.

Tomorrow, after the pilgrim service at the great cathedral of Santiago, I will take a bus on to Finisterre and finish what I set out to do: burn my pills. After this symbolic act, my Camino will be formally complete. I head over to the cathedral leaving my cheer section behind. *Enjoy Santiago, amigos, and thank you very much for the clapping. It was touching.*

It's a long way through the city, but I take my time. I stroll along in the sunshine like an Olympian doing a victory lap. It is a beautiful city, and I march through it with my head held high. The cathedral is breathtaking. I drop my pack and sit in the middle of the square. I need nothing to savour this moment. I take one photo of my boots and one of the cathedral. I decide not to go inside just yet, because I don't want to rush this experience. I will save it for tomorrow.

When I'm good and ready, I make my way to the pilgrim's office and receive my Compostela. I start to cry. I stare at it for a moment. It's my moment. The lady behind the counter smiles at me, but I cannot say anything. I turn and go. Earlier I had walked into a fancy hotel which is what I thought I had wanted, but found myself turning around and walking out again. I don't know what has gotten into me, but it seemed all wrong; a return to the "other" world too soon. I want my own room so I can reconcile my thoughts, but it felt too lux and garish; it disgusted me. I have spent the last month in noisy albergues, but I didn't stop being a pilgrim when I walked into Santiago. I don't want to waste money on something inauthentic. I had been dreaming of this very thing for 800 km and it turned out to be not what I wanted at all. *So what the heck DO I want?*

VICTORY LAP

> At the center of your being,
> You have the answer;
> You know who you are
> And you know what you want.
>
> –LAO TZU

As I leave the pilgrim office, a lady with bright, happy eyes asks me in perfect English, "Where do you want to stay in Santiago?" I step back in shock because she's just read my mind. I really don't know where I want to stay, so I stammer back, "Somewhere nice. My own room with a key so I can come and go." "I have one room left across the street with a giant room that has two balconies for €23. It has shared bathrooms and I can do your laundry in the morning for you." I can't get my wallet out fast enough.

Montes is directly across from the pilgrim office in the square of the Museo de Pilgrims and 100 meters from the cathedral. It's central to all the shops and nightlife. It turns out to be exactly what I want. I drop off my backpack and hit the street. I stop at a happening local bar and order a giant plate of paella. Paella is a rice dish with saffron, giant mussels, shrimp, calamari served with fresh warm bread. I eat and drink as much as I can take. It is 4:30 pm and the night is young. I wander the streets for hours and stock up on local cheese and wine, and purchase a terracotta cup, a bottle opener, jamon, and crackers. I may not want to go out later at all, let alone party, so I should stay prepared. Hunger is never far away when you're a pilgrim, and being prepared has become second nature.

I thought I would want to dance and let loose tonight, and maybe I will... tomorrow. I have a few days to see the city. For the first time, I'm in no rush at all.

Buen Camino, Heather.

I put my feet up and take a selfie photograph.

I enjoy the early evening sitting on my balcony drinking beautiful wine, eating amazing cheese and crackers, watching the bustle of people pass below. I hear the church bells at 7:30 pm calling pilgrims to mass. I will definitely go before I leave.

By 8:30 pm I'm done with my thoughts and want to get out and see more of Santiago. I feel rested and tipsy, but I want to celebrate in style. I walk the streets alone for about an hour. I look into shop windows but see nothing I want to buy or carry. The atmosphere is sizzling and there are people everywhere. It's magical. There are couples holding hands, stopping for a kiss or some sweet embrace. Everyone seems to be in love. My heart feels a pang of loneliness pass through it and I wish I was holding someone's hand too.

I have to remind myself that I'm in Santiago! And to be honest, I'm feeling pretty darn good about things. I run into the two old Finnish fellows I had been trailing for days. They ask me to go for a drink and I accept. These boys can really hold their liquor. I probably should slow down on the drinking, but we stop at several bars and have a glass of wine in each one. I order a plate of fresh mussels with a salsa sauce for us to pig out on. They taste incredible; fresh from the sea.

I bump into other pilgrims I know, and part with the Finns. I chat with two men I had hiked with for a little while today: Paco and Eduardo. Both of them are from Spain and have a combined knowledge of about 1% of the English language. Predictably, communication is accomplished by cheers, hand gestures, and smiles.

Eduardo is beautiful to me: tall and muscular, and I'm thinking how maybe I might like to hold his hand for a little while. And so, after a few more glasses of wine, an interpreter pilgrim helps me and Eduardo to have a conversation. The interpreter sits with us on the ground outside of a bar, patiently translating for hours. Eduardo suggests that I go back to his hotel and take a bath with him. I reply that "it's not possible because I haven't shaven my legs today." The interpreter says to me, "Heather, it's really just a simple yes or a no." I concede because Eduardo is so handsome. We walk off into the night together, holding hands and stopping for passionate kisses along the way. It's all right out of a movie.

I am not thinking about anything but how happy I am. We behave like all young lovers do and practically run to his hotel. I can't wait. What a way to celebrate my first night in Santiago, and is it so wrong to celebrate my last day of cancer treatment with relish? I tell myself that I absolutely deserve a one night stand!

Eduardo is a passionate and exciting lover. I am not disappointed. He's affectionate and I could crown him tonight as the best kisser and lover I have ever had. I wish I could bottle up Mr. Eduardo and take him home with me. We now have no interpreter but we hardly need one. He holds me in his arms all night kissing my cheeks and my lips. His hands roam my body, sending electric tingles all through me. It is ridiculously sensual. This is my first EVER one night stand, and I have to say, I highly recommend it! I can't believe I will have to say goodbye soon. His plane leaves this morning and I creep out around 8:30 am to start my walk of shame. With the tenderest of goodbyes, we part. What a delicious man! Would it be laughable to sell everything and move to Spain?

I find my hotel after some difficulty, and tiptoe into my untouched room. I'm exhausted and hungover, but I have the biggest stupid grin on my face.

CHAPTER 35

Pilgrim Mass

DAY 35 November 1

(Santiago)

I can barely lift my head when as promised, the hospitalero opens my door at 9:30 am to take my laundry. I've been "home" for 45 minutes. She tells me I should get out there and enjoy the day. My head plunks the pillow as I answer, "If I keep enjoying the days as much as the nights, I'll be in big trouble." I get up at 11:00 am. Pilgrim's mass is at noon, so I had better get moving. My only prayer at the moment is to not vomit inside the cathedral.

I slide into a pew beside the old Finns. They ask me how my night was. How on earth should I answer that? I'm sure my face says it all but I mumble "not too bad at all." I see the interpreter in the pew ahead of me. He grins at me and winks. I lift a finger to my lips and breathe *shhhhh*. He zips his lips in acknowledgement.

The church is filling up with so many familiar faces. It's really very touching. Gerhild slides in next to me just before the service begins and I confess my latest sin to her. She finds my confession fantastic and is doubled over in silent laughter. So far no one has pointed a gnarled finger at me or shouted, "Heretic!" The service is held by 3 men clad in red robes, a nun, and a man in a brown robe who may have been a monk. I wish I knew more about the Catholic church to better understand their roles. The service is carried out with absolute precision and the singing is celestial. A priest acknowledges the pilgrims in a special way by calling out the countries that have arrived in Santiago. I hear "One: Canada," and I realize that it's for me. The church is so beautiful that my eyes scan the room taking mental snapshots. I try hard to listen, but the service is in Spanish and with the echo from the microphone, it sounds more like Spanish underwater. My thoughts travel back to Eduardo and our night together. It doesn't feel like a sin at all because I have joy surging through my veins.

Three men hoist a large incense ball into the air with thick ropes and let the ball swing down through the aisle between the pews. I breathe in the scent and feel eternally blessed.

Before long, the service seeps into my pores and I get choked up and shed a few tears. I have enjoyed my Camino and take time now to consciously and deliberately thank God for my life; for sparing me. I hope there will be a space for me in Heaven when the time comes. I believe there will be.

I see Flavio, Vicki, and the Portuguese man. I nod in their direction and give them a wide smile. It's my opportunity to say a proper goodbye to Flavio, which absolves my guilt for ditching him. There is no discussion about our "losing" one another before entering Santiago; there is only understanding. We embrace and wish each other well with our lives. He is leaving for the airport right away, so our goodbye is a brief one. With a flourish of the Brazilian flag, Flavio the Great makes his exit. Bye, bye, sweet Flavio. Bye, bye.

And all's right with the world.

Gerhild and I decide to go for something to eat with another pilgrim from Switzerland. While we're sitting outside the bar I see two of my trail children from Korea. What a surprise, I had thought they were long gone. They ask me where Roberto is, but I actually have no idea. I was kind of wondering the same thing, myself. They want to visit Canada and I tell them my door is always open.

PILGRIM MASS

I try again to see the *Museo for Pilgrims*, but it seems perpetually closed. I take a tour of the church instead, to say hello to Saint James. He has a very nice coffin, for the record. It's very ornate and shiny. I guess I should be feeling something right now because I have walked a long way to see him. I don't. I'm coming up empty. It doesn't *feel* like the Apostle James is in there at all. I fleetingly wonder if it is his real resting place. I don't feel cheated. I realize that it doesn't matter to me if he is in there or if he isn't. The point is he existed. The real energy is on the trail. I came all this way for God... and I feel *Him* everywhere.

Afterward, I find myself in the tacky cathedral gift shop. I surprise myself by buying a rosary. *For whom? Myself? I'm not even a Catholic. Is this something I want to have in my home? Nope. I will give it away. That's it. But for whom?* In the moment, I don't understand why I buy it at all, but I trust the instinct. I buy a cookbook as well. This is what I'll enjoy most when I return home. I love to cook! I surprise Gerhild with a matching bracelet with a rosary and a cross. We are twins.

Gerhild and I are staying in separate hotels but we will meet for dinner, and in the morning we are taking a bus over to Finisterre. There is talk of going to Muxia as an added bonus, but it doesn't seem as important as Finisterre; for either of us. I can't imagine spending an entire day on the bus just to say I've been somewhere.

Dominic, Gerhild and I, along with another pilgrim whose name I didn't catch, meet up with Gord and Monica from Toronto for a bite to eat. I feel rude forgetting names, but names just don't matter as much as the experience. We eat an incredible meal at a recommended restaurant that is relatively easy to find. And no, I didn't catch the name of the restaurant either. I'm in the moment, here!

The last thing I want is *more* wine, so I order a *beer* though I can't even finish it. My plumbing needs a rest. Spain is so social that it's hard not to get right back in the saddle. I decide to go easy on the alcohol and try something foreign and probably not all that digestible. I choose their famous *pulpo* (octopus) with spicy paprika and coarse salt, which is delicious. Dry toast is for babies.

The restaurant windows in Santiago really pull you in with sides of beautiful beef, whole octopus, platters of mussels, shrimp, and other unidentifiable ocean things. I think wistfully, *where is my casa by the sea? How can I live six months in Spain and six months in Canada? Is a life like that possible for me? Who says a Canadian snowbird has to fly to Florida. I love the food here, the culture, the lifestyle, the walking, and the sea.* My mind is working overtime. We say our goodbyes, and I am like a horse running for the barn to my hotel. All of this fun is incredibly exhausting!

CHAPTER 36

End of the World

DAY 36 November 17

(Santiago to Finisterre +/- 100 km by bus and car back to Santiago)

Gerhild is at my doorstep at the crack of dawn, as promised. We wait for our friend Chris, from Africa, who has agreed last minute to join us. This is wonderful because I still have his tupperware from the day we met. I tell Gerhild if he doesn't show up I will burn it for him at the cross. Alas, he does arrive, and we head over to take a bus... that will take us to the bus station. It's obvious that no one wants to walk anywhere anymore. We grab a quick coffee and chocolate croissant to fortify us for the long 3 hour bus ride. I have brought my fancy purse; a purple mesh laundry bag filled with wine, snacks, and my Tamoxifen medication, along with 1 tupperware. We gather a few other pilgrims along the way, one of whom is a German sweetheart named Suzanna, and we spend the day together. The day is bright and sunny, but we aren't fools: we keep our rain gear at the ready.

Pilgrims learn preparedness, but no one has brought their bathing suit. *Why didn't I think of this?* Well I did, but it was the first thing to get mailed back to Canada, back in St. Jean Pied de Port. Honestly, who would swim mid-November anyway? A crazy Canuck would; it's my birthright to polar dip through icy waters.

The bus ride is sublime. We are sitting on the top of a double decker bus enjoying the ocean view. *Is that my future house by the sea down there?* I relish the view whenever I'm not falling asleep bonking my head against the window pane. I'm still a baby when it comes to wheels turning; five minutes and I'm out like a light. If you ever want to shut Heather up for a little while, take her for a drive around the neighbourhood.

I'm in love with Finisterre, but any of these coastal towns will do. *Is this my life right now? Somebody pinch me.* What's fitting about the Camino is that it doesn't give out its secrets for free. Every one of them is earned. And so, the bus doesn't drop us off at the end of the world; there is a 6 km round trip up a mountain to the cross. The coastal view helps with the hike and we can hear the crash of the oceans waves below us. There are fishing boats, flowers in bloom, and orchards of lemon, apple, and orange. We walk past a Spanish market and browse the novelties for sale. No one buys anything. At the top of the mountain, I open up the wine. I brought with me a small terracotta cup that I fill with wine and pass around. Like communion. There is a man standing by the cross and I hail him over to us.

Mario, our newcomer, takes a sip of the wine. He just happens to be a winemaker from Sardinia and it has been a bad year for wine. He says that every year is different; some good and some not-so-good. He had only a few days of vacation so he decided to get away to Santiago for some relaxation. He says he would have loved to have walked the Compostela, but it is hard to get away from his work. He is shy and seems enormously touched that someone has thought to bring wine. It is, after all, the one thing he is trying to forget. He empties the cup as an afterthought; to remember and to forget as it were.

We take a number of photographs, but we still need to find the "burning place". We hike on. At the very top of the mountain I can hear the repetitive crash of the waves against the craggy rocks below. The whoosh and whish of the wind creates a quiet but noisy atmosphere; if that makes any sense. The burning place has a concrete cross also and a small sitting area. There is no one around; no one to care that we are setting boots, pants, shirts, socks, and medicine on fire. The fire lights without much difficulty, despite the wind, and within seconds, our sins and sorrows are ablaze. I take one more Tamoxifen pill for good luck and wash it down with a mouthful of wine. I sprinkle the rest of the pills over the fire and toss in the blue prescription bottle. That Heather is gone. The new, healthier Heather is stronger in body, mind, and spirit.

I watch our things shrivel up before casting alight; tears are flowing freely down my cheeks. I look to the sky and marvel the expanse. It's just one moment of many, but it has taken my lifetime to get here.

The experience is humbling and powerful. Each of my new friends hugs me one by one. They are witnessing an important moment in my life, and in return, I am witnessing theirs. We are silent. We stare at the raging fire, lost in our own thoughts, marking the end of each of our Caminos.

With the last piece of the puzzle completed, we feel lighter, cleaner, and freer. Mario speaks first. "I have a car!" We cheer collectively. He offers us a ride back to Santiago, as it would be faster than taking the bus. We accept, probably a little too quickly, but I get the sense our presence is helping Mario in a deeper way. It is the smallest car I have *ever* seen, but we all manage to pile in helter-skelter... after the necessary hike down the mountain. We race back to Santiago in no time at all, grateful we aren't arriving at what would have been 10 pm by bus.

> Joy has taken over the entire town,
> even the sky and the earth are in bliss.
> Only sorrow is complaining
> because You have freed everyone from it.
>
> –RUMI

It's only 4:30 pm and we're starved. We go out for supper, and eat paella and drink beer. It's another rowdy night, though not as late as last night. In that regard I'm on my best behaviour. We naturally run into fellow pilgrims: Monte, Angele, a Belgian man with his German girlfriend, Cameron, a redheaded surfer from California, and the list goes on.

Chris (S.Africa) leans over and covertly tells both Gerhild and I that he is gay. It's not a secret to us, but we let him talk. I say, "So Chris, I had a one night stand last night". It breaks the ice and he giggles with glee. He's simply in love with the bartender who is wearing a purple t-shirt and is likely half his age. Good for him. Gerhild discreetly takes the bartender's photograph from under her armpit and says she will forward it to Chris later on. Chris has a look of Christmas morning wonder on his face at the prospect.

We bar hop, eating tapas and drinking all night, until Gerhild and I look at one another cross-eyed. She is staying in a spare bed in my hotel room tonight, and we stagger home holding each other up.

Gerhild is covered in bed bug bites. I've managed to avoid all of that by some miracle. Everyone seems to have them. Aren't these critters hard to get rid of? I vow to leave my backpack outside all winter when I get home. Night, night, Gerhild... Stay on your side!

CHAPTER 37

The Pilgrim's Shell

DAY 37 November 18

(Santiago to France)

I leave tonight at 10:00 pm. It's strange, but after seeing Finisterre, I'm ready to go now. Yes, of course I will miss everyone, but there are only a select few of these faces I will ever see again. Gerhild is one of them. If she lived in Canada, I would hang out with her all of the time. She is so easy to be around. Her sense of humour is dry like my own, and we have become Camino sisters.

So… little bit of a headache this morning. *Groan*. It takes roughly a millennium to shower, pack up, and get my lagging ass out the door. Gerhild says I can leave my backpack at whatever hotel she decides to get today until I'm ready to leave for the train station. Perfect, because it's pouring buckets.

We make it five whole steps from Montes Hotel before we stop for a coffee to wash down our Ibuprofens. We can't decide what to do for the day. We consider a museum or something, but we change our minds when we meet some trail friends and decide to enjoy their company instead. Chris, who is leaving for Barcelona, is among them. He tells us over coffee and pastries that last evening was the most fun he's had in 23 years. I'm delighted for him. Yesterday was the most fun I've had in 2 days, but I don't mention it. I think of Eduardo and I tell Chris he absolutely MUST get laid in Barcelona.

Dear God, please help this man get loved and laid!

Gerhild and I leave Chris to go shopping for leather purses. We want to get one like Suzanna's for €20, which is unheard of back home. We never do find the place where she bought hers because the market booths are closed due to the rain. We continue to look in every store, but come away empty handed. Finding a small bag is something of an emergency for me because I need something to carry my passport, wallet, etcetera, on the plane. It just might end up being a plastic bag to add more value to my vagabond look. Nobody was ever going to mistake me for Julia Roberts anyway.

Some pilgrims are gathering at 6 pm at the cathedral to get drinks and supper. I see Angele and Roberto, who has just arrived, and we embrace for a hug. He tells me he has walked every step of the trail, and I gush with pride for him. Gerhild and I suggest a pre-drink before the scheduled pre-dinner drinks. I inform Roberto that the Korean boys have inquired about his progress and that they in return have made it to Santiago in one piece. We cheers our beers and then Roberto has to go and find a place to sleep tonight. We girls continue our shopping and find a few treasures. We spread the word to every pilgrim we see about meeting at the cathedral at 6 pm. I can hardly wait to take a group photograph.

The onslaught of pilgrims gathering is really something to see, and my eyes scan over the many faces that I have come to know and love. Never again will we all be together, but we are united forever in our memories. I wish I could stay the whole evening, but I've got a train to catch. I take the time in the courtyard to talk to as many pilgrims as I can. There is a flurry of photos, exchanging of emails and addresses, and the atmosphere is both happy and wistful.

The crowd has drinks together. I see Co slip into the bar and drift over to me. I haven't seen him in weeks. He kneels by my chair and speaks to me quietly. He has just arrived to Santiago and is exhausted. I know he won't stay long because he hasn't found a place to sleep yet. He had heard from other pilgrims I was here, and he wanted to see me. He looks both *lost* and *found*. I take his hands in mine and look into his face and say to him, "Co, I realize it's possible that I'll never see you again, but I want you to know that I shall never forget you." I kiss his cheek and hug him good-bye. I will also never forget the sweet look on his face. That look, sums up our complete and utter appreciation for one another. I know I had to be wearing the exact same expression.

After a time, the merriment of the bar becomes overwhelming, and a few of us drift away for dinner. Pauli, Roman, Gerhild, and I slip off together, to use our remaining minutes in meaningful conversation. We order pulpo, mussels, and the like. Gerhild contorts her face in disgust at the seafood. She is a chicken-and-potatoes kind of gal; with beer con limon. We champion our way through two bottles of red wine and stay for a lovely dessert. Oh man, it's already time to go home. A gut wrenching sadness looms over us, but what can be done? Gerhild walks me to get my things. She's ready for an early night anyhow. She gives me a small package and tells me to open it on the train. We hug and I start bawling as my taxi drives away. Oh Gerhild, you are such a lovely person. I will miss you so much!

I have three trains to get to Biarritz, France. It's going to be a long 24 hours, and then I'll have a short rest before I head back to Canada. I'm ready for home completely, but thoughts of home haven't flooded back into my head yet. Mentally, I'm still in Santiago. I feel a bit differently now, after having been weeks away from home. I'm an altered version of Heather. I suspect life at home will still be rolling along in a similar fashion, which in some ways will be wonderful; in other ways, it'll be a difficult transition for me. Re-emersion will be like fitting a large circle into a tiny square.

I open Gerhild's gift. It's a pilgrim's shell. I read the letter stuffed inside it and know everything is as it should be. I guess this is both my friend and the universe telling me I have *earned* my shell.

Like all good things that come to an end, so did the Camino. The healing and lessons learned seem to still linger in the air like an invitation; another beckoning stone for the pilgrim. This may be the end of one trail, but it feels like the beginning of another.

My gratitude pilgrimage taught me to live as authentically as possible. It's easy to fall into step with what others want from us. We can lose ourselves without even realizing it, which doesn't serve anyone. If you can stay true to who you are, then you will have more love to give. The more love you give, the more you will get in return; like a karmic boomerang. Staying true to who you are is fundamental. It helps you to be able to tune into what your needs are in order to rejuvenate and deliver your best in life. If you are depleted, then you will eventually become ineffective in your own life and have nothing to give to others or the things you are passionate about. It can be a gerbil wheel. That brings me to the importance of tenderness, love, and care towards ourselves and others. Sometimes we forget to do both because it is awfully hard to do.

Judging ourselves and others is second nature to most of us; myself included. Let's face it, judgement is offensive and hurtful; it's a bad habit and it adds nothing to our lives. Our thoughts, our actions, and our words are powerful instruments that we should not wield carelessly. Being mindful of our words with others shows an intention to communicate in a genuine way. Meaningful relationships need this to survive. Whenever I am feeling in the mood to judge someone I try to see that person as a soul that is more than just their body. That makes it easier for me to have compassion for them.

This pilgrimage has taught me a beautiful recipe for how to live life well. Body, Mind and Soul = Balance. I believe that if this balance can be attained and nurtured even just a little, it will open the gateway for a more fulfilling life. It's a challenge, and it's something that requires work. Some days we will fall far from the mark, but our intentions will be noticed. Our only celestial expectation is to get up, dust ourselves off and try again.

So what about love? I know that everyone deserves love. I for one am ready to receive love from a loving partner. If and when I am healed, he will materialize in my life. I have thankfully experienced the real kind of spiritual love here on the Camino and it made me feel safe and warm. I am clearer now about what I want and need in my everyday life. I'm certain that I will recognize authentic love when it crosses my path going forward.

I have to believe there's somebody out there waiting, for someone exactly like me. I wish this for you also.

The Compostela delivered everything to me that it was supposed to. It beckoned me to re-live the last ten years of my life, step by blistery step: a failed marriage, a transition to Canada to build a new life, a critical illness, broken relationships, and being without a space of my own for several years; my perseverance in the face of adversity, my stubbornness to live, and my courage to endure it all with a gritty sense of humour. I've even managed to tone down the negativity a notch. Somehow through everything, I've experienced hope, joy, gratefulness, tenderness, and a budding self-love. You really just can't get a better bang for your buck.

It has been, and continues to be, a buen Camino! What more could anyone ask for?

Afterword

People have asked me time and time again, "So what did you do with the stone that Sue Kenney gave you at the film festival? Did you leave the stone along the Camino somewhere special? Is it in Santiago now? Finisterre?" And my personal favourite: "Did you mail it back to Sue?" For some reason, I never took it with me at all; it hadn't even occurred to me to bring it back to the trail. The answer to the question is this: The stone must have accomplished its purpose, because I can't for the life of me find it anywhere. It has simply vanished.

There was never a Camino reunion.

Grizzly met someone while I was away, and a few years later married her. I met my life partner, Sean, 6 months after my return from Spain.

Gerhild did find us leather purses like Suzanna's the day after I left Santiago, and she mailed one over to me in Canada. I returned the favour and mailed her the grocery store perfume.

And strange, come to think of it, I never did see one Honda the entire time I was in Europe.

Special Thanks

It took a small village to make me into a pilgrim. For starters, I want to thank the Universe for letting me live. I am truly humbled and grateful.

Special thanks to all the pilgrims I met along the trail to Santiago who taught me invaluable lessons, showed me love, laughter and million other little things that I will never forget.

Thank-you to Sue Kenney, you are a mentor and my friend. You listen patiently and fill me up with hope and possibility during each and every interaction that I have with you. You pulled me out of darkness with the gift of stone. To Elizabeth Racic, without your gift of free tickets for film festival, I would have not seen the film *Las Peregrinas: The Women Who Walk*. To Denise and Ken Tellier, who lent me your vehicle that had a copy of *My Camino* on the front seat.

Thank-you to my medical team: Dr. Olivier, Dr. Brule, Dr. Robinson, Dr. Shehata, for getting me well. There are also countless nurses and ancillary staff who played their very important roles to perfection. To each and every one of you, I take a bow. You made the whole 'experience' easier for me.

For whom I cannot say enough! To my completely *amazing ninja of an Editor Stephane Cervone*, You allowed me to keep my *voice!* Without your help and encouragement this book could have easily remained at the back of my closet in the form of a journal.

Thank you to my extremely talented cousin Daryl Graham for your clever design and art contribution of the sketched shell. I realize that this was something you could have drawn when you were 4, but I'm still glad it was you who did it for me. Muuuaaaahhhh xo!!

To Mary Oliver for her books of poetry that grace every single room in my home and for her permission to use my favourite poem "The Journey".

To Maryam Mafi, who is the kindest woman I have ever known. Without a blink of an eye, she granted me permission to use her beautiful Rumi translations and wrote a lovely endorsement for my book. Rumi has been in my blood for decades and was most certainly with me on my pilgrimage. Having access to these works was important to me for so many reasons and Maryam made that dream into a reality. I am touched by your generosity and will be looking for an opportunity to pay it forward.

To *The Mother Teresa Center*, specifically SR. M. Callisita, I give thanks for your guidance in researching the most appropriate quote and providing those resources to me. Permission to use the inspiring words of Mother Teresa was a humbling gift of charity to receive. Mother Teresa has been my hero since I was a child, which makes it even more spectacular to have her blessing.

To Diane Conway, thank you for your support, beautiful endorsement and for introducing me to my amazing interior and cover design team, Studio 6 Sense. Diane you gave me tools and poignant advice at the right time. So Diane, I am grateful for your honesty; along with the large helping of confidence. Thank-you!

To my sweet Auntie Pauline, thank-you for your patience when reading one of the very early drafts of this book. And, being the teacher that you are, made some corrections in bright red ink for me. Thank-you also, for the many positive comments and suggestions that helped me sculpt this manuscript.

To my friends in Canada who helped get me organized for my trip (before, during and after) I will say this: I am lucky to have you in my life! A hearty thanks for keeping everything going while I wandered off for weeks at a time. To Margaret Ferrucci, for selling me a lot of Euros the day before I left on my trip because the bank didn't have any. To Julie Sauve, who fetched me at the airport at midnight upon my return home and helped me celebrate my return with a beautiful bottle of red wine. To Amber Konikow, Joe Hurban and Adam Lassaline, who house sat and cared for my pets during my prolonged absence. I really can't thank-you all enough.

Thanks to Grizzly, for the good and the bad. To my unique family, from whom I have learned the most, and last but never least, my life partner Sean, who is my soft place to land and my best friend.

Bibliography

Goethe, Johann Wolfgang von. Public domain.

Mafi, Maryam; Kolin, Azima Melita. "Rumi's Little Book Of Love". Charlottesville, VA: Hampton Roads Publishing Company, Inc. 2009 pgs. 9,11,43,59,101,113 (print).

Oliver, Mary. "Dreamworks". New York, NY: Atlantic Monthly Press Books, 1986. pg. 38 (print).

Teresa, Mother. "Where There Is Love, There Is God". New York, NY: Doubleday Religion, an imprint of the Crown Publishing Group, a division of Random House, Inc. 2010 pg. 311 (print).

Tzu, Lao. Public domain.

Ward, William Arthur. Copyright and/publication information unable to be determined, despite extensive research.

Biography

Heather Gauthier is a full-time critical care nurse with a Bachelor's of Science in Nursing, and a Masters in Business Administration. A breast cancer survivor herself, she has raised thousands of dollars for breast cancer research and supportive care over the years. She is a singer-songwriter with one CD titled, *A Miner's Song,* from which 100 % of the proceeds are donated to an education fund for the son of a Sudbury miner who lost his life on the job. She lives in Northern Ontario with her partner Sean, their two dogs, Noosh and Clegg, a macaw named Gonzo, and a horse named Tucker. **The Pilgrim's Stone** is her first nonfiction book. She is currently working on her second book titled ***A Cabinet of Curiosities***.

CHAPTER 38

The REAL Last Chapter

Transformation

With the Camino's end, I returned to Canada as the Christmas season was beginning. I had difficulty adjusting to the commotion of lavish Christmas parties, dresses and money allocated to whims of fancy; all of which, I might add, I used to take part. None of it was important to me anymore and I didn't want to participate in any of it. I went inward and isolated myself as I tend to do in times of confusion and kept the details of my journey to myself.

I found the dichotomy between the pilgrimage and the return to my real life to be so drastic that I fell into a dormant phase that lasted nearly 5 years. I felt like a misfit. I slid into gluttony and gained 30 pounds, continued smoking, and walked the razor's edge when it came to drinking. I felt empty and exhausted and wondered how it had come to this. Once again, I knew I was on the sidelines of my life but felt powerless to move forward in a healthy and productive way. I functioned normally and worked full time, but my life seemed stalled and stagnant.

I recognized the signs and symptoms of early-stage cancer starting to return, but told no one. It frightened me and I knew that I had been cavalier with my lifestyle. I feared changing my bad habits, but I dreaded a second round of cancer treatments more. I was spending a lot of my time sleeping, instead of hiking and running. I stopped planning things with friends because I wasn't sure how I would feel on any given day.

I didn't feel vibrant or excited, but instead felt similar to how I had the year before I was diagnosed with breast cancer. Back then I had attributed my fatigue to stress, but this time I had no stress and was living a quiet and peaceful life. I was certain from the daily signs and symptoms that physical issues were manifesting and that Western science hadn't detected it.

I decided to give myself a short window for self-healing before I would see a doctor to get more tests done. It was a risky move seeing as my brother was imminently dying from stage 4 cancer and both my parents had recently fought their own battles with cancer. I was almost too exhausted to make the necessary changes in my life, but I knew that if I didn't, I was going to be in big trouble. I had been in this very place before and I was at least smart enough to know the universe was asking me to *pay attention*.

Without a second thought, I knelt before my soul and asked for clarity and guidance. I took a blind chance on a friend's recommendation to have energy work done. I didn't realize *how* out of balance I was and how all of this was affecting me physically until the healings began and my healer confirmed my suspicions. There was never any judgement or disappointment during these healings; I was encouraged to implement new ways of doing things that would serve me better. It was both humbling and empowering, and instead of allowing myself to be devastated, I took charge and bolted into action.

I recommitted to meditation, specifically Kundalini Yoga, with a new vigour. I continued to ask my body to heal itself and to forgive me for abusing it so badly. I felt synergy and flow return to my systems and as my chakras began to align and open, the kundalini began to rise; this time at my own pace. I switched to an alkaline diet and tempered my other bad habits. I conceded that more green vegetables in my diet couldn't be a terrible idea when the alternative might be another battle with cancer; a battle that I might not win a second time around.

Almost immediately I felt less congested, my allergies and mental fog disappeared, and I slept deeply. I felt the pain in my body shift for a few days until it eventually disappeared. I was actively participating in the removal of the shackles of my pain and suffering. Without the daily chronic pain, I wanted to get outside again and walk. I wanted to breathe fresh air and connect to the earth in some way. I felt more alive than I had in years and it was inspiring. It was a tremendous effort which catapulted my life in a new direction. I felt like a pilgrim again.

It was hard to believe that a month prior I didn't think I could keep working full time as a nurse and was contemplating a part time job. Now, I felt my inner power returning and I realized THAT was why I couldn't speak about my experience when I first came back; I needed to wait until I could tie all of the peace, love, and harmony together. I had to be able to speak about healing myself from the heart so that it would be clear to myself as well as others.

Despite all of these new changes, I still had absorbing, healing, and strengthening to do. I simply could not find the courage to share the soul-shaking aspects of my journey without out publicly exposing my weaknesses as well. I worried about judgement from others; real or imagined. I still felt raw and beautifully vulnerable.

I finally began speaking about my experience with trusted spiritual seekers in my life who had specifically asked to hear about it. I felt honoured to share in a way that wouldn't be forcing anything on anybody. They had *asked* me. Finding the courage to speak about these important lessons of my experience presented me with the opportunity to re-live the Camino. I was able to *re-learn* what I had so effectively pushed down for safe-keeping. I had become an active participant in my healing and truth, and I felt passionate about getting my life back on the spiritual path.

Listening to myself speak for the first time from the depths of my heart gave me the impression that my higher self was speaking to my lower self, and that part of me that needed love and support. I was *finally* strong enough to stand on my own two feet and hold my ground without fear. I wanted to share what I had learned about tenderness and self-love now that I was more in tune with my body, mind and soul.

I realize now that I hadn't wanted to just tell stories about what had happened. I had gone inward and became dormant because I still had learning and integration to do. With these recent changes I felt more supported, which allowed me to see the bigger picture. It seemed selfish for me to continue doing self-destructive things; to continue doing harsh things to my body out of "pleasure-seeking," given the eventual consequences that I could have faced. The well being that I was experiencing in my life became all that I needed to continue moving forward in a healthier manner: body, mind and soul. I felt incredible with these few easy changes and there was no going back. Overnight, I had simply lost my desire to live like I had been. It was high time to take control of my life in a more positive way and help anyone along the way that was interested.

People began asking me what it was that I was doing differntly. I hadn't realized that there was anything to notice. After some thought I did what I always tend to do and blurted out the truth. In turn, others shared with me what they were doing to make positive change in their lives. A dialogue has begun, which I hope continues as we have much to learn from one another. It turns out that there is a student and a teacher in all of us.

And so, The Pilgrim's Stone ends the same way it began: I am a pilgrim; we all are.

Made in the USA
San Bernardino, CA
29 March 2018